COLLECTOR'S GUIDE TO

TOOTSIETOYS

THIRD EDITION

Identification & Values

BY DAVID E. RICHTER

COLLECTOR BOOKS

A Division of Schroeder Publishing Co., Inc.

Cover design: Beth Summers
Book design: Joyce Cherry

Cover photo designed and constructed by David E. Richter.
Photographs by David E. Richter

Tootsietoy® is a registered trademark of the Strombecker Corporation.

Should you have any comments on the information in this book or have Tootsietoy items available for sale, you may write to David Richter, 6817 Sutherland
Ct., Mentor, OH 44060.

Searching For A Publisher?

Contents

Acknowledgments

Special thanks first to my wife, Jean, for her support, understanding, and helpfulness once again with my new third edition of *Collector's Guide to Tootsietoys*. She helped with the proofreading and made several good suggestions to make this book a success.

I would like to thank my brother, Danny, for the good times we had at toy shows we attended through the years and for spotting great Tootsietoys I may have overlooked at toy shows.

Many thanks to all the antique dealers and toy dealers I wrote or talked with in person at various shows. I would like to thank many collector friends for supplying me with a photo of a toy I didn't have in my personal collection. They are not in any special order, Steve Ozonwich, Hans Stang, Steve Butler, and Gates Willard.

A special thank you goes to Myron B. Shure, past chairman of the Strombecker Corporation, for his permission to do this new book and use the Tootsietoy product name throughout my text.

Finally, thanks to William Schroeder of Collector Books, Gail Ashburn, the editor of Collector Books, for her continuous support, all the many book dealers who carried and sold my value guide, and all those who wrote with new valuable information.

Preface

I would like to welcome you to my new revised third edition of Collector's Guide to Tootsietoys. This new edition has many new chapters and toys not pictured in my last edition. The Wheel and Tire Identification is all new, showing 36 of the most common types of tires and wheels used on Tootsietoys along with a brief description of each. All the rare 1959 Chevrolet cabs pulling their trailers are pictured in one chapter. To date none of these trucks appear in any book with their trailers. Yes, these rare trucks do exist and are very hard to find.

Prices were averaged from some auctions results, selling prices at local toy shows, and dealer display ads in many of the toy publication papers and magazines. My brother Danny and I attend as many shows as we can to find that toy we need to fill a void in our collections. I also upgraded or added many Tootsietoys to my collection. It often seems that all collectors need the same piece.

The first Tootsietoys were produced around 1910 by a company called Dowst. Tootsietoys are still produced today under the Strombecker Corporation name.

Toys in their original packaging and boxed sets are much sought after by serious collectors. Tootsietoy made thousands of boxed sets over the years. The question is how many survived and have come on the market today. I am amazed that a collector would pay $750.00 for a Transamerican bus at a recent auction. I often wonder if prices of other collectible items and Tootsietoys will ever level out.

My wife, Jean, also likes to attend many types of shows with me. She is searching out that bargain kewpie doll, Longaberger basket, Barbie doll, or Pez dispenser that she doesn't have in her collections. At any rate the fun is in the search, trying to spot a rare toy or item at a reasonable price at any show.

I hope you enjoy reading and looking at the hundreds of toys in this value guide.

In the future I plan on writing a separate book on the Tootsietoy doll furniture and metal miniatures.

I welcome your comments and letters about any toys not covered in my text.

History

Strombecker is the oldest toy company in the United States, dating back to 1876. The Dowst Brothers Company was started to publish the National Laundry Journal. They made the collar button and several different laundry accessories.

Samuel Dowst in 1893 saw a new type-casting machine located at the World's Columbian Exposition. He recognized the possibility of making molds to cast the collar button from lead or similar type metal. The start of the die-cast industry was born thanks to his success with making molds for the collar button.

The evolution toward Tootsietoy products continued to prosper rapidly. Many miniatures were made for various industries — miniature flat irons, shoes, skillets, plus many more. These trinkets were gathered together and sold to the candy industry as prize items to be put in their penny packages. This great effort by Dowst was the start of a strong toy die-cast process.

The year 1914 saw the first successful toy production: Henry Ford's very famous Model T. Around 50 million attractively packaged Tootsietoy Model T's were produced. Tootsietoy is a name that has continued today to dominate the die-cast toy industry with its many attractive packaged toys and their excellent realism.

The Tootsietoy name applied to only some of their die-cast products. It wasn't until after a Dowst brother had a granddaughter named Toots, they decided to name the doll furniture toys after her. The trade liked the name so well it was adopted for all of the company's die-cast toys.

The Cosmo Manufacturing Company was established by Nathan Shure in 1892, to make small novelties for Cracker Jack and other candy firms — a similar business to the Dowst Brothers Company. In 1926, the two die-cast giants merged calling their new company, Dowst Manufacturing Company. They produced many replicas of the various GM models, Fords, and other popular cars on the road at that time. Tootsietoy was seeing a great need to appeal to the youngsters and besides its realistic brightly painted cars, decided to add doll furniture, train sets, farm sets, and airplanes of that era to its line.

The children who played with Tootsietoy products not only grew up, but passed their enthusiasm to not only their children, but their children's children.

The large demand for all the various Tootsietoy products grew so rapidly that a new modern plant was constructed to meet the demand for their attractive and varied items.

In 1961, Shure's descendants purchased Strombeck-Becker, makers of electrically-powered plastic cars. Henceforth, the company adopted the Strombecker name and is still called Strombecker Corporation today.

Toy collecting today is a very popular hobby, enjoyed by many serious collectors of all age groups. Tootsietoy vehicles are among the most sought after and are quite valuable to collectors today. Quite a number of Tootsietoys that were once bought for five and ten cents are now between $50.00 and $100.00 and up.

I personally think Tootsietoy products are not only great toys for children and collectors now, but will be preserved and passed on for generations to come.

How to Use this Guide

Chevrolet Panel Trucks, 3"

Beside or under each photograph within this guide you will find the following information: the catalog number of the Tootsietoy shown, the name of the toy, the year the toy was made, and the years it appeared in various catalogs. An example is 1950 – 1960. Prices are given for toys in each of the following three conditions:

The first truck on the left is an example of a toy with about 90% of its original paint. This toy is fine having only small paint chips and all its tires on its axles.

The middle truck is an example of a toy with about 95% of its original paint and only slight wear on the tires and high points of the toy's body.

The last truck on the right is an example of a toy with 100% of its paint. This toy should have no tiny imperfections or chips. These toys in mint state will bring you a better return for your money down the road.

Tootsietoy Value Guide

90% — Fine, having only small paint chips and at least 90% of the original paint on the body.

95% — Slight wear on tires and the high points on the body. This toy should have at least 95% of the original paint on the body.

100% — No imperfections or chips and having 100% of paint. The last price being brand new or in an absolutely mint state.

Please note that almost all of the Tootsietoys from 1970 to 1979 have several decals or stickers on them. Please take into consideration the condition of decals and stickers when purchasing a piece for your collection. If possible, upgrade your set or collection when a mint piece comes along. Like other collectibles, the best condition will bring a high price in the future when reselling your items or toys.

Wheel & Tire Identification

Tootsietoy has produced thousands of transportation and military vehicles with all types of tire and wheel combinations. Metal, rubber, wood, and plastic were used; only the 1936 – 1941 Midget Series had its non-moveable wheels within the casting of the toy. I would like to expound on several of the most common types to further your knowledge of America's first die-cast toys. The first type of wheel was a small open-spoked metal wheel used on the 2" No. 4528 Limousine.

Wheel type No. 1 – These were used on the No. 4528 Limo, 1911 – 1928; the No. 4482 Bleriot, behind the wing on the World Flyers toy planes of 1925; Passenger train set No. 4626 and No. 4627 Freight set cars.

Wheel type No. 2 – These were used primarily on the airplanes: No. 4660 Aero-dawn of 1928, No. 4675 Bi-wing plane, No. 106 Low Wing, and No. 107 High Wing of 1932. The earlier Ford Tri-motor planes had gold or purple painted wheels with matching props like the other examples listed. Early passenger and freight train sets had this wheel, usually painted to match the color on the train cars.

Wheel type No. 3 – These were used on all the 2" toys in the 100 series of 1932. The only exception was the No. 108 Caterpiller that had grooved wheels with rubber treads placed on them.

Wheel type No. 4 – This was a slightly larger cast solid spoked wheel than No. 3. They were only used on the No. 4655 Ford Model A coupe, No. 6665 sedan, and the unnumbered U.S. Mail Ford van sold in sets 1931 – 1933 only.

Wheel type No. 5 – A larger open spoked wheel was used on the No. 4570 Ford Tourer from 1914 to 1923 and the No. 4610 Ford pickup from 1916 to 1923. All the earlier train engines had four spoked moveable wheels painted black and the other wheels were within the toys casting.

Wheel type No. 6 – A solid clincher type metal wheel was used on 3" cars and trucks from 1914 to 1932. Some examples were Model T's, Federal vans, Mack truck series, and of course, all the different GM series 3" models. It was painted gold to begin with and later painted black.

Wheel type No. 7 – A tiny white rubber tire was used only on the No. 119 Army plane of 1936.

Wheel type No. 8 – A slightly larger white rubber tire than No. 7 was used only on the 3" vehicles. It was introduced in 1935 and used on these toys until 1941. Trains and airplanes produced between 1933 and 1941 had these tires.

Wheel type No. 9 – A small metal hub that had a white rubber tire mounted on it was used on all 1934 Ford models and wreckers. These wheels were used on 1928 Fords, GM series, and several other 3" toys in 1933 that are very hard to obtain today. The No. 196 and No. 197 Tootsietoy Flyer trains of 1937 – 1941 used these wheels on the three-piece train units. The hub without the tire was used on all Buck Rogers rocket ships in 1937 for the string to glide on.

Wheel type No. 10 – A black painted clincher wheel like No. 6 was used on the 3" vehicles of 1931. Examples are the GM series vehicles, Mack Army gun trucks, and searchlight trucks to name a few.

Wheel type No. 11 – A black painted solid disc wheel was used on the later no-name series GM vehicles. I've seen examples on Army gun and Army searchlight 3" toys.

Wheel type No. 12 – This wheel had a white rubber tire on its rim and was primarily used on all the Jumbo series vehicles from 1936 to 1941 including the Transamerican bus of 1941.

Wheel type No. 13 – A small black rubber tire was mounted on a landing wheel support on several airplanes of the 1950s. Examples are Boeing 707 of 1958, Stratocruiser, and Constellation. Earlier smaller jets used this type of tire also. The wheel supports were part of the plane's casting of the body.

Wheel type No. 14 – Small black rubber tires were used on many 3" cars and trucks from 1947 to 1960. The tires were put on many prewar toys that were reissued after the war. Almost all airplanes and trains produced between 1947 and 1960 had these rubber tires.

Wheel type No. 15 – The larger rubber tires were on 4" and 6" vehicles of all sorts from 1947 to 1960.

Wheel type No. 16 – These wheels had black rubber tires with a tread-like appearance. I've seen them on various 4" military cannons and vehicles. Others may exist though.

Wheel type No. 17 – This white rubber tire on a solid hub was on most 4" toys from 1933 to 1941. Examples are Grahams, La Salles, larger Mack semis with single and dual rear axles, No. 810 Wrigley's Gum trucks. Some vehicles used a blind hub on the passenger side of the toy. It held the wheels on by a nail passing through body loops to the back of the blind hub.

Wheel type No. 18 – The larger white rubber tire with its chrome tin cap really dressed up Tootsietoys. Examples are No. 1040 Fire truck series, all the Jumbo vehicles, No. 1046 Woody wagon, and No. 1010 Wrigley's Gum truck.

Wheel type No. 19 – A small plastic wheel with the Tootsietoy logo appeared around 1955, replacing the smooth rubber tires. These tires were used on some train engines and train cars in the late 1960s and early 1970s.

Wheel type No. 20 – This plastic tire with built-in spokes was first used on the 4" Ford LTD car. Trailers of this period used these tires well into the 1970s.

Wheel type No. 21 – The treaded tire of plastic replaced the smooth black tire. They appeared on toys around 1955 and were used on 4" vehicles and several different trailers into the early 1970s.

Wheel type No. 22 – White and black wood wheels appeared on several 4" vehicles issued without trim silver paint. The Jumbo series vehicles also can be found with both colors of wood wheels. My best estimate is that wood was used in 1942 and 1946.

Wheel type No. 23 – The larger plastic tires had Tootsietoy embossed on the outer rim on both sides. They replaced rubber tire No. 31 on all 6" cars, Mack trucks, and semi tractors with trailers.

Wheel type No. 24 – This black plastic tire was similar to No. 23, but a had different tire tread pattern and a simulated hubcap cast with the molded tire. The tire was on a few 5" racers, 6" toys, and semi tractor front wheels.

Wheel type No. 25 – The smallest of the Tootsietoy tires without the company logo was on the HO series semis of the 1960s and 1970s. All Jam Pac vehicles, the four jets from 1970s, and the unmarked No. 2855 Diesel train used these unmarked tires.

Wheel type No. 26 – The fat plastic tire was used on Tiny Toughs from 1975 to 1979 and the three highway vehicles of 1976 – 1979.

Wheel type No. 27 – This larger spoked wheel was used only on the No. 0191 Contractor set's three dump carts. They were either painted red or green.

Wheel type No. 28 – The plastic tire pictured with its plastic white rim was used on almost all 4", 6", and 9" tractor and trailer semis. Vehicles from 1969 to 1979 had this type.

Wheel type No. 29 – These hollow back plastic tires with silver trimmed hubcaps were used on the 1980s toys.

Wheel type No. 30 – The six spoked metal wheel was used on No. 4654 Farm tractors with and without rear trailer hooks, all four wheels on the roadscraper 1928 – 1932, and the rare No. 4654 Army tractor with ammo box behind its seat.

Wheel type No. 31 – This black rubber treaded tire with sidewall details of a real car tire was excellent. It can be found on early 6" cars, jeeps, trucks, and larger semi trucks.

Wheel type No. 32 – The purple plastic wheel was used on the Tootsietoy Playmates vehicles from 1970 to 1972, the No. 2019 Delivery Truck series of 1971, and on similar mid-sixties vehicles of the styles above.

Wheel type No. 33 – The large painted spoked wheel was on the 1931 – 1940 Long Range cannon only.

Wheel type No. 34 – The largest black six-spoked rubber tire was used on only a few toys. Examples are later No. 4642 cannon, rear tires of the rare No. 1011 tractor, and front tires on large Ford tractors of early 1950s.

Wheel type No. 35 – The largest metal six-spoked wheel was used on the rear axles of the early farm tractors and the Army tractor only. It was painted many different colors to go with the many color schemes of the toys. All four wheels should be the same color.

Wheel type No. 36 – Two wheels cast onto a small axle at different lengths were used on all prewar ships and the two types of Coast Guard seaplanes only.

I hope the photo and descriptions will help you as a collector or dealer to better identify the most common Tootsietoys wheel types.

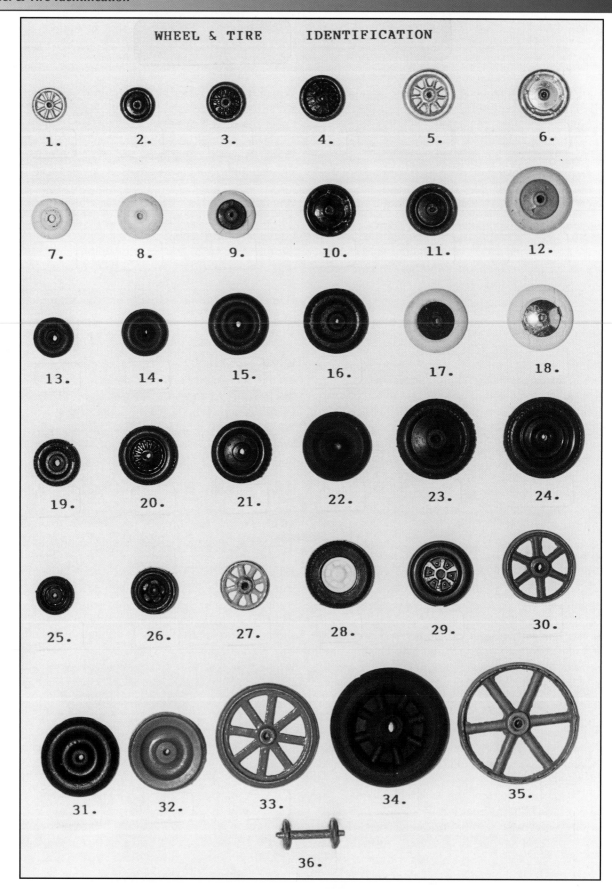

WHEEL & TIRE   IDENTIFICATION

1. 2. 3. 4. 5. 6.

7. 8. 9. 10. 11. 12.

13. 14. 15. 16. 17. 18.

19. 20. 21. 22. 23. 24.

25. 26. 27. 28. 29. 30.

31. 32. 33. 34. 35.

36.

Note: Tires are actual size.

Aircraft and Spaceships

The first Tootsietoy plane, No. 4482 Bleroit, was issued around 1910. The earlier version of the small 67mm plane had small spoked wheels — later models had the solid disc type wheels. The tiny No. 4650 with its match-like crossed struts to support the wings was issued in 1926. The small yellow and red plane is quite scarce today and is probably well underrated in price. It was only produced just a few years in the 1920s.

The No. 119 Army plane of 1936 is one of the most common pre-war era planes. It came in assorted colors and later around 1939 – 1941 was even camouflaged. Camouflaged planes of all types are quite scarce today and sure would be a welcome piece to anyone's collection.

Tootsietoy No. 722 the DC-4 Super Mainliner appears as not only a silver civilian liner, but as an Army Transport and the really scarce Tootsietoy DC-4 camouflaged Bomber. The Transport and Bomber were camouflaged in tan and green, and also light blue with tan. The latter is more rare.

The Navion and the F-94 Starfire, for the most part, are the most common postwar planes. They are available at all your local toy shows and flea markets.

I would say almost all of the various types of airplanes pictured in this chapter were placed in boxed sets with other airplanes or with accessories such as small three-piece baggage carts, loading ramps, tiny die-cast pilots, and badges of various airlines with their names on them.

No. 4482 Bleriot Plane
1910
$100.00/$125.00/$150.00

No. 4650 Biplane
1926
$125.00/$135.00/$150.00

No. 4660 Aero-dawn
1928, early wheel type
$75.00/$90.00/$105.00

No. 4660 Aero-dawn
1934
$70.00/$85.00/$100.00

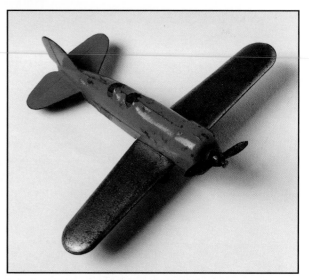

No. 106 Low Wing
1932
$85.00/$95.00/$105.00

No. 107 High Wing
1928
$85.00/$95.00/$105.00

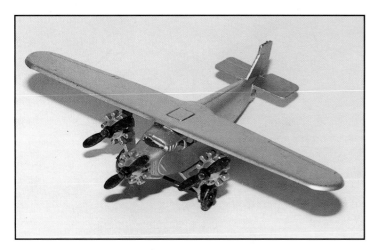

No. 4649 Ford Tri-motor
1932, early wheel type
$125.00/$135.00/$150.00

No. 4649 Ford Tri-motor
1932
$125.00/$135.00/$150.00

No. 4675 Bi-wing Seaplane
$75.00/$95.00/$105.00

No. 4675 Bi-wing plane
1934
$90.00/$100.00/$110.00
early metal wheels
$70.00/$85.00/$100.00

No. 4660 Seaplane
$70.00/$85.00/$100.00

No. 4659 Autogyro
1934, early wheel type
$115.00/$125.00/$140.00

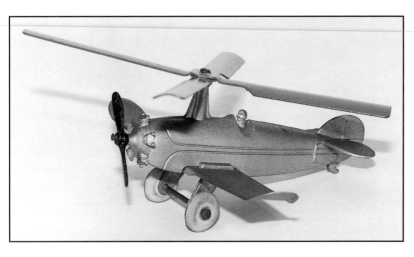

No. 4659 Autogyro
1934
$110.00/$120.00/$135.00

No. 720 Fly-n-gyro
1938, rare
No price available

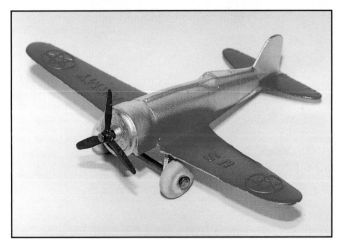

No. 119 U.S. Army plane
1936
$75.00/$95.00/$105.00

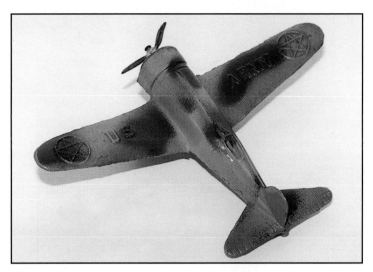

No. 119 U.S. Army plane
camouflaged
$80.00/$100.00/$110.00

No. 717 DC-2 TWA
1937
$85.00/$95.00/$105.00

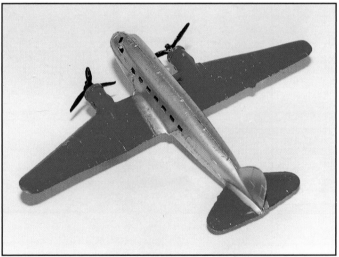

No. 717 DC-2 TWA
1942 – 1946, two-tone
$90.00/$100.00/$110.00

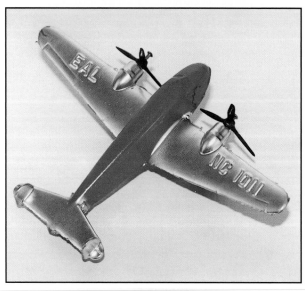

No. 718 Waco Bomber
1937
$105.00/$125.00/$140.00

No. 125 Lockheed Electra
1937
$75.00/$95.00/$105.00

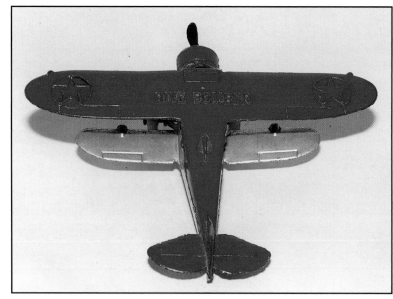

No. 718 Waco Dive Bomber
1937, sets only
$145.00/$160.00/$175.00

No. 718 Waco Dive Bomber
1941, camouflaged, rare
$150.00/$175.00/$200.00

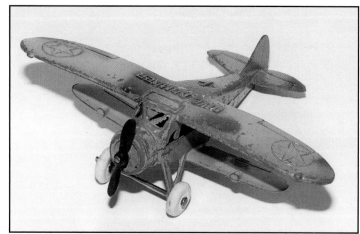

No. 719 Crusader
 1937
$105.00/$120.00/$135.00

No. 1030 Dirigible Los Angeles
1937
$120.00/$130.00/$140.00

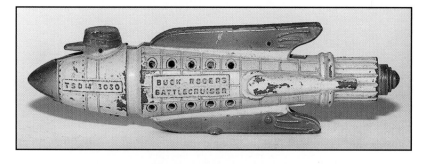

No. 1031 Buck Rogers Battlecruiser
1937
$120.00/$130.00/$140.00

No. 1032 Buck Rogers Venus Duo-Destroyer
1937
$120.00/$130.00/$140.00

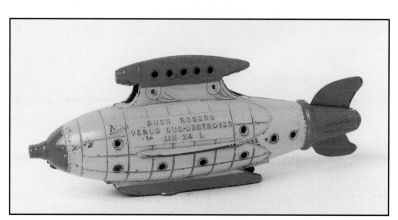

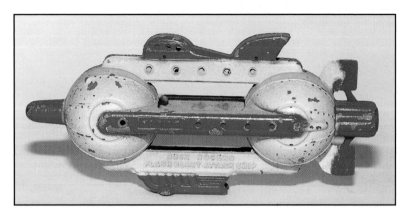

No. 1033 Buck Rogers
Flash Blast Attack Ship, 1937
$120.00/$130.00/$140.00

No. 721 Curtis P-40
1941, red stars
$200.00/$225.00/$250.00

No. 721 Curtis P-40
1941, white stars
$200.00/$225.00/$250.00

P-80 Shooting Star
1948
$30.00/$35.00/$40.00

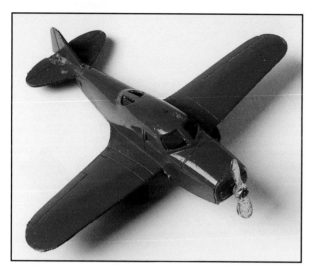

Piper Club
1948 – 1962
$20.00/$25.00/$30.00

Piper Cub
1948 – 1952, closed windows
$25.00/$30.00/$35.00

Navion
1948 – 1953
$20.00/$25.00/$30.00

Navion
1948 – 1953, closed windows
$25.00/$30.00/$35.00

Beechcraft Bonanza
1948, cast prop pin
$35.00/$40.00/$45.00

Army Bonanza
1948, note decals
$40.00/$45.00/$50.00

Beechcraft Bonanza
1950
$20.00/$25.00/$30.00

Twin Engine Convair
1950
$85.00/$95.00/$105.00

Twin Engine Convair
1958 – 1959, sets only, two-tone
$100.00/$110.00/$120.00

Coast Guard Seaplane
1950, early version
$120.00/$150.00/$180.00

Coast Guard Seaplane
1950s, two-tone
$110.00/$140.00/$170.00

F 86 Sabre Jet
1950, two-piece body
$20.00/$25.00/$30.00

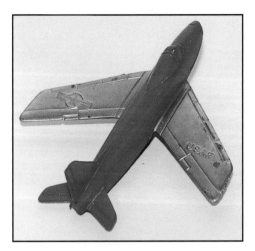

F-86 Sabre Jet
1956, one-piece body
$15.00/$20.00/$25.00
Note: Above also in OD paint w/star decals
$20.00/$30.00/$40.00

Panther Jet
1953 – 1955, two-piece body
$25.00/$35.00/$45.00

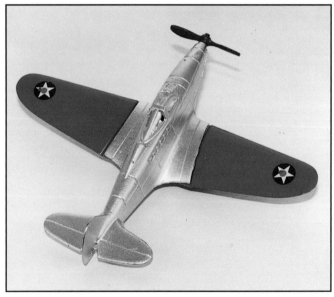

Army Panther Jet
1953 – 1955, one-piece body
$30.00/$40.00/$50.00

P-39 Fighter
1947, early version, rare
$140.00/$180.00/$225.00

P-38 Fighter
1950
$105.00/$115.00/$125.00

P-39 Fighter
1947, later version
$110.00/$140.00/$175.00

Boeing Stratocruiser
1951 – 1954
$105.00/$115.00/$125.00

Lockheed Constellation
1951
$115.00/$130.00/$145.00

Delta Jet
1954 – 1955, rare
$30.00/$40.00/$50.00

Panther Jet
1956 – 1969, one piece-body
$15.00/$20.00/$25.00

F-94 Starfire
1956 – 1969
$15.00/$20.00/$25.00

F-94 Army Starfire
1956 – 1969
$25.00/$35.00/$45.00

Navy Cutlass
1956 – 1969
$15.00/$20.00/$25.00

Army Cutlass
1958 – 1960
$25.00/$35.00/$45.00

F-40 Skyray
1956 – 1969
$15.00/$20.00/$25.00

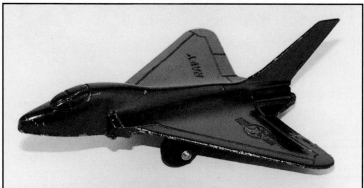

F-40 Army Skyray
1956 – 1969
Note: Above sold with and without star decals on wings
$30.00/$35.00/$40.00

United DC-4 Super Mainliner
1941
$90.00/$110.00/$130.00

United DC-4 Super Mainliner
1941, camouflaged
$100.00/$120.00/$140.00

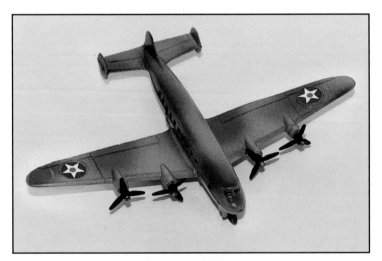

"Army" DC-4 Transport
1941, camouflaged
$100.00/$120.00/$140.00

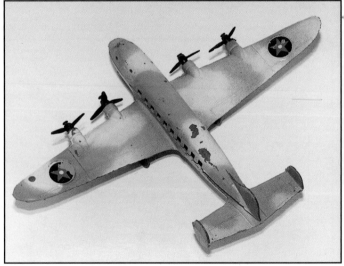

DC-4 Long Range Bomber
1941?
$175.00/$200.00/$225.00

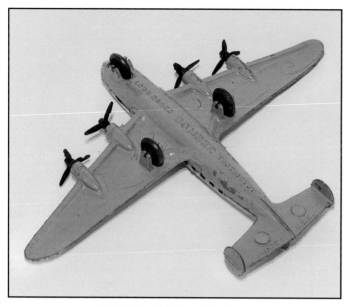

DC-4 Long Range Bomber
(bottom)
$175.00/$200.00/$225.00

Boeing 707
1958
$45.00/$55.00/$65.00

Hiller Helicopter
1968 – 1969, rare
Blades metal, plastic
$95.00/$110.00/$125.00

Sikorsky S-58 Helicopter
rare, Blades metal, pastic
$110.00/$125.00/$140.00

Sikorsky S-58 Army Helicopter
sets only, rare
$115.00/$135.00/$150.00

Barclay plane with piggyback Tootsietoy Midget St. Louis
1936
$50.00/$75.00/$100.00

Bleriot Plane
The World Flyers Toy
1925, 1 of 4 planes
red, blue, green, yellow
No price available

No. 5100 Airport Hanger
1931, came with two Tri-motor planes
missing air sock
$150.00/$175.00/$200.00

Automobiles and Racers

The first Tootsietoy auto was the small No. 4528 Limo produced around 1911. It came in black, dark blue, and dark green. Early examples of this model had tiny spoke-type wagon wheels trimmed in gold. In later years, the wheels were all painted black. This toy, like a few other earlier toys, was not marked by the company.

Lincoln Zephyrs, La Salles, and the Graham series cars and vans are really tough to locate for sale — especially in mint condition. The above pre-war toys were nicely detailed with their own shiny metal grills and bumpers along with white rubber tires mounted on their own rims.

The rarest post-war model in the three-inch series would still be the Nash Metropolitan convertible. The rarest four-inch postwar, I think, would be the 1941 Chrysler Windsor convertible. The rarest six-inch series would be the 1950 Chrysler with its delicate windshield still in place.

Since my book's first printing I have managed to upgrade almost 95% of my vast Tootsietoy collection to mint or near mint models. Hope you enjoy this new expanded chapter on Automobiles and Racers. Elsewhere in this book, you will find separate chapters on just the Graham models and the GM series models of the 1920s and 1930s.

No. 4528 Limousine
1911 – 1928, 2"
$40.00/$55.00/$70.00

No. 4570 Ford Tourer
1914 – 1923, spoke wheels
$50.00/$60.00/$70.00

No. 4570 Ford Tourer
1924 – 1926, disc wheels
$45.00/$55.00/$65.00

No. 4629 Yellow Cab Sedan
1921 – 1933
$40.00/$45.00/$55.00

No. 4636 Buick Coupe
1924 – 1933
$50.00/$65.00/$80.00

No. 4641 Buick Tourer
1925
$50.00/$60.00/$70.00

No. 4655 Model A Coupe
1928
$45.00/$55.00/$65.00

No. 6665 Ford Model A Sedan
1928
$50.00/$60.00/$70.00

No. 23 Small Racer
1927, rare
$65.00/$90.00/$115.00

No. 101, 102, 103, 110, 2" models
1932
$35.00/$45.00/$55.00

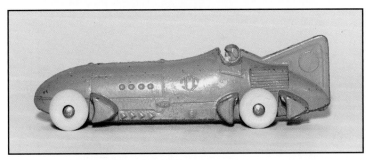

No. 4666 Large Bluebird Racer
1932 – 1941
$40.00/$55.00/$65.00

No. 4666 Large Bluebird Racer
1932 – 1941, game piece
Number on fin 1 – 8, metal, rubber,
tires on hubs wheel types
$50.00/$65.00/$75.00

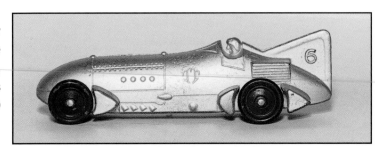

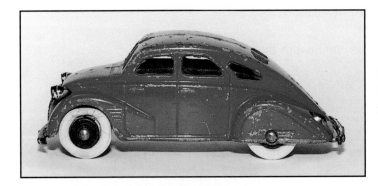

No. 716 Doodlebug
1935 – 1937
$85.00/$100.00/$115.00

No. 0712 La Salle Coupe
1935 – 1939
$140.00/$190.00/$260.00

No. 0713 La Salle Sedan
1935 – 1939
$140.00/$190.00/$260.00

No. 0714 La Salle Convertible Coupe
1935 – 1939
$145.00/$195.00/$265.00

No. 0715 La Salle Convertible Sedan
1935 – 1939
$145.00/$195.00/$265.00

No. 6016 Lincoln Wrecker
1937 – 1938
$225.00/$295.00/$375.00

No. 6015 Lincoln Zephyr
1937 – 1939
$225.00/$295.00/$375.00

No. 6016 Lincoln
1937 – 1938, windup, rare
Tin bottom base plate
$225.00/$295.00/$375.00

No. 0112 1934 Ford Coupe
1935
$70.00/$85.00/$100.00

No. 0114 1934 Ford convertible Coupe
1935
Note: Rare color combo
$75.00/$90.00/$105.00

No. 0111 1934 Ford Sedan
1935
$70.00/$85.00/$100.00

No. 0115 1934 Ford Convertible Sedan
1935
$75.00/$90.00/$105.00

1935 Ford Convertible Coupe
rare
$85.00/$110.00/$135.00

1935 Ford Convertible Sedan
rare
$85.00/$110.00/$135.00

No. 111 1935 Ford Sedan
$45.00/$55.00/$75.00

No. 112 1935 Ford Coupe
$45.00/$55.00/$75.00

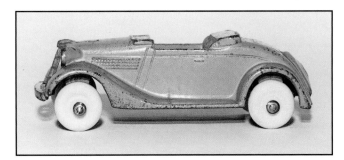

No. 116 1935 Ford Roadster
$50.00/$60.00/$80.00

No. 0118 DeSota Airflow
1935 – 1939
$55.00/$65.00/$80.00

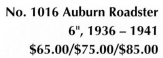

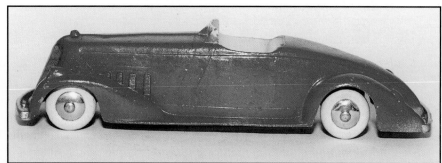

No. 1016 Auburn Roadster
6", 1936 – 1941
$65.00/$75.00/$85.00

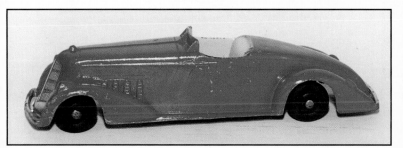

No. 1016 Auburn Roadster
6", 1942 – 1946
$45.00/$55.00/$65.00

No. 1017 Jumbo Coupe
1936 – 1941
$45.00/$55.00/$75.00

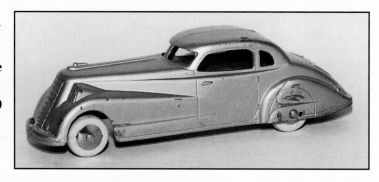

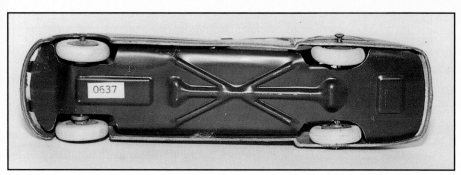

No. 1017 Jumbo Coupe
1936 – 1941, tin bottom
$65.00/$75.00/$95.00

No. 1017 Jumbo Coupe
1942 – 1946
$40.00/$50.00/$70.00

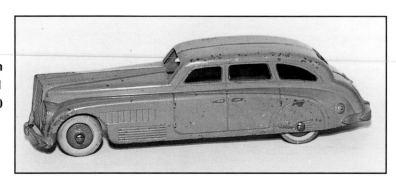

No. 1018 Jumbo Sedan
1936 – 1941
$45.00/$55.00/$75.00

No. 1018 Jumbo Sedan
1936 – 1941, tin bottom
$65.00/$75.00/$95.00

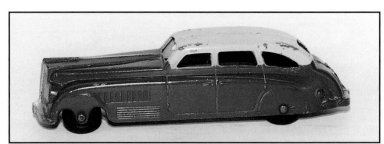

No. 1018 Jumbo Sedan
1942 – 1946
$45.00/$55.00/$65.00

No. 1043 Ford & Trailer
1937 – 1941
$65.00/$85.00/$105.00

1935 Ford Fire Chief Car
1938 – 1940, sold in sets only
$140.00/$190.00/$240.00

No. 230 La Salle Sedan
3", 1940 – 1941
$35.00/$45.00/$55.00

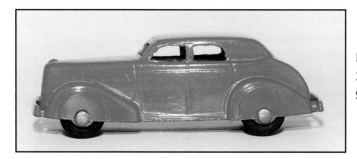

No. 230 La Salle Sedan
3", 1947 – 1952
$30.00/$40.00/$50.00

No. 231 Chevy Coupe
1940 – 1941
$30.00/$40.00/$50.00

No. 231 Chevy Coupe
1947 – 1952
$30.00/$40.00/$50.00

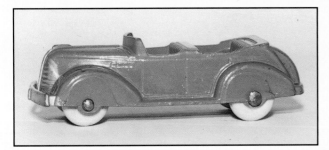

No. 232 Open Touring
1940 – 1941, rarest in series
$45.00/$55.00/$65.00

No. 232 Open Touring
1947 – 1952, black tires
$40.00/$50.00/$60.00

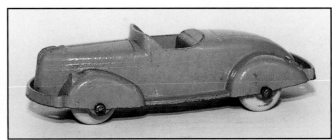

No. 233 Boat Tail Roadster
1940 – 1941
$35.00/$45.00/$55.00

No. 233 Boat Tail Roadster
1947 – 1952
$25.00/$35.00/$45.00

No. 239 Station Wagon
1940 – 1941
$40.00/$50.00/$60.00

No. 239 Station Wagon
1947 – 1952
$25.00/$35.00/$45.00

1956 Austin-Healy
5", 1959 – 1964
$35.00/$45.00/$55.00

1954 Buick Station wagon
6", 1955 – 1959
$40.00/$45.00/$50.00

1954 Buick Experimental
6", 1958 – 1964
$45.00/$50.00/$55.00

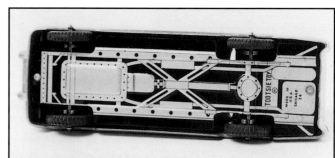

Buick Experimental
Note: Detailed tin bottom, rare
$65.00/$70.00/$75.00

1951 Buick XP-300
6", 1953 – 1959
$45.00/$55.00/$70.00

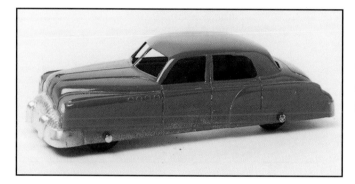

1949 Buick Roadmaster
4-door, 6", 1949 – 1950
$45.00/$55.00/$65.00

Buick Estate Wagon
6", 1948, open grill
$80.00/$90.00/$100.00

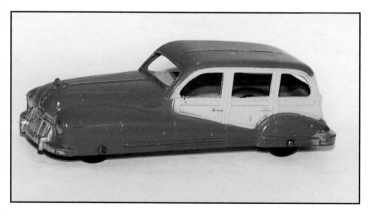

Buick Estate Wagon
6", 1948, closed grill
$80.00/$90.00/$100.00

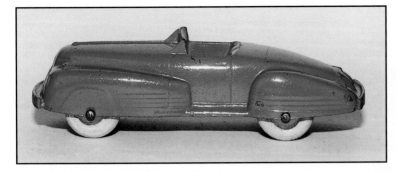

1938 Buick Roadster
4", 1942 – 1946, wood wheels
$45.00/$55.00/$65.00

1938 Buick Roadster
4", 1947 – 1949
$40.00/$50.00/$60.00

1948 Cadillac 60
4-door, 6", 1949 – 1954
$35.00/$45.00/$55.00

1954 Cadillac 62
4-door, 6", 1955 – 1959
$40.00/$50.00/$60.00

1954 Cadillac 62
4-door, 6", 1955 – 1959
tow hook model
$45.00/$55.00/$65.00

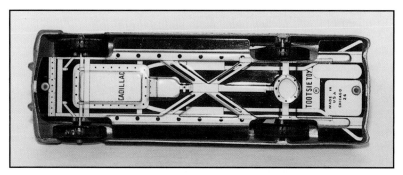

Cadillac 62
Note: Detailed bottom, rare
$65.00/$75.00/$85.00

Chevy Fastback Coupe
4", 1942 – 1946, wood wheels
$45.00/$55.00/$65.00

Chevy Fastback Coupe
4", 1947 – 1949, rubber tires
$35.00/$45.00/$55.00

Chevy Fastback Coupe
4", rubber tires
Note: No fender trim
$40.00/$50.00/$60.00

1955 Chevy Bel Air
3", 1956 – 1958
$20.00/$25.00/$30.00

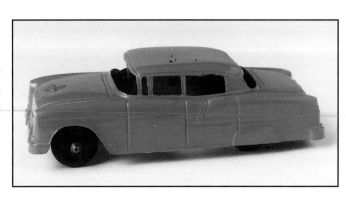

1950 Chevy Fastback
3", 1951 – 1954
$20.00/$25.00/$30.00

1953 Chrysler New Yorker
6", 1953 – 1954
semi-rare, rare two-tones
$75.00/$100.00/$125.00

Chrysler Experimental Roadster
6", 1947 – 1949
$40.00/$50.00/$60.00

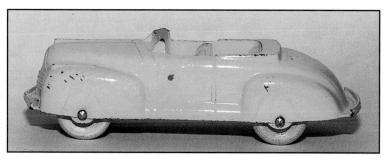

1941 Chrysler Windsor Convertible
4", 1942 – 1946, wood wheels
$45.00/$55.00/$65.00

1941 Chrysler Windsor Convertible
4", 1947 – 1949
$35.00/$45.00/$55.00

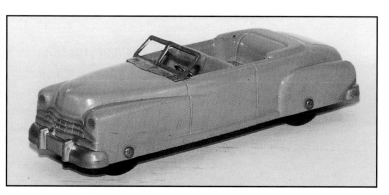

1950 Chrysler Windsor Convertible
6", 1951 – 1955, rare
$100.00/$125.00/$150.00

1960 Chrysler Convertible
4", 1961 – 1964
$20.00/$25.00/$30.00

1956 Ferrari Racer
6", 1960s
$35.00/$45.00/$55.00

No. 1046 Station Wagon
4", 1940 – 1941
$55.00/$70.00/$85.00

No. 1046 Station Wagon
4", 1947 – 1949
$55.00/$65.00/$75.00

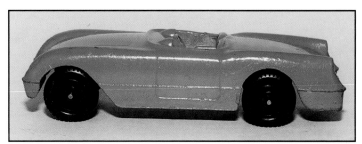

1954 – 1955 Corvette Roadster
4", 1955 – 1969
$25.00/$35.00/$45.00

1931 Ford B Hotrod
3", 1961 issue
$20.00/$25.00/$30.00

1949 Ford Convertible
3", 1949 – 1954
$25.00/$30.00/$35.00

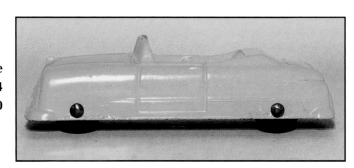

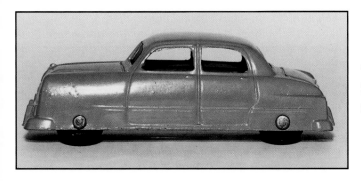

1949 Ford Sedan
3", 1949 – 1954
$25.00/$30.00/$35.00

1952 Ford Mainliner
4-door, 3", 1952
$30.00/$35.00/$45.00

1955, Ford Customline
3", 1955 – 1958
$25.00/$30.00/$35.00

1957 Ford Fairlane 500 Convertible
3", 1959 – 1969
$20.00/$25.00/$30.00

1954 Ford Ranch Wagon
3", 1955 – 1960
$25.00/$30.00/$35.00

1954 Ford Ranch Wagon
4", 1955 – 1960
$30.00/$35.00/$40.00

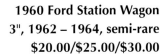

1959 Ford Ranch Wagon
6", 1959 – 1967
$30.00/$35.00/$40.00

1960 Ford Station Wagon
3", 1962 – 1964, semi-rare
$20.00/$25.00/$30.00

1962 Ford Station Wagon
6", 1964 – 1968
$25.00/$35.00/$45.00

1960 Ford Falcon
3", 1961 – 1964
$20.00/$25.00/$30.00

1940 Ford
6", 1960 issued
$45.00/$55.00/$65.00

1960 Ford V-8 Hotrod
6", 1959 – 1969, with & without tow hook
$25.00/$30.00/$35.00

1960 Ford V-8 Hotrod
6", Note: Detailed tin bottom, rare
$65.00/$75.00/$85.00

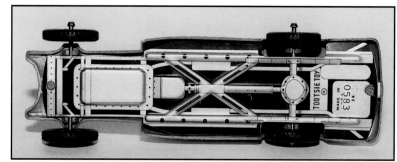

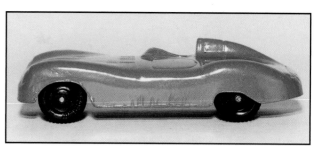

1969 Ford LTD
4", 1970
$20.00/$25.00/$30.00

1957 Jaguar Type D
3", 1959 – 1960
$20.00/$25.00/$30.00

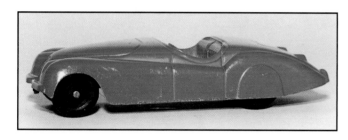

1954 Jaguar XK 120
3", 1955 – 1960
$20.00/$25.00/$30.00

1954 Jaguar XK 120
3", 1964, plastic
Colors: Red, blue, green
$10.00/$15.00/$20.00

Jaguar XK 140 Coupe
5", 1959 – 1969
$25.00/$35.00/$45.00

1947 Kaiser Sedan
6", 1947 – 1949
$45.00/$55.00/$65.00

1956 Lancia Racer
6", 1960s
$30.00/$40.00/$50.00

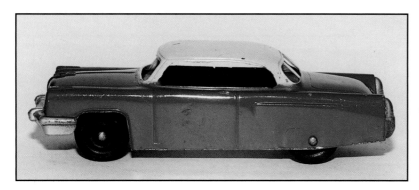

Lincoln Capri
2-door, 6", 1953 – 1958
$30.00/$40.00/$50.00

1956 Mercedes 190 SL Coupe
5", 1959 – 1964
$30.00/$40.00/$50.00

1949 Mercury Custom
4-door, 4", 1950 – 1952
$30.00/$40.00/$50.00

1949 Mercury Fire Chief Car
4", 1953 – 1960
$40.00/$50.00/$60.00

1952 Mercury
4-door, 4", 1953 – 1954
$25.00/$35.00/$45.00

1954 MG TF Roadster
3", 1955 – 1960
$25.00/$30.00/$35.00

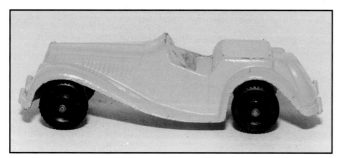

1954 MG TF Roadster
3", 1955 – 1960, open fender wells
$25.00/$30.00/$35.00

1954 MG TF Roadster
5", 1959 – 1967, no tow hook model
$30.00/$40.00/$50.00

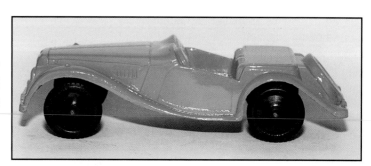

1954 MG TF Roadster
5", 1959 – 1967, tow hook model
$30.00/$40.00/$50.00

No. 2015 MG TF
Tubby Teddy, 5", 1966,
rare with head
$75.00/$100.00/$125.00

Nash Metropolitan
2½" , 1954, rare
Note: Two axle variations
$65.00/$85.00/$100.00

1947 Offenhauser Racer
4", 1947 – 1969, rubber & plastic tires
#3, #5, #7, #8 known
$20.00/$25.00/$30.00

1949 Oldsmobile 88 Convertible
4", 1950 – 1954
$30.00/$35.00/$40.00

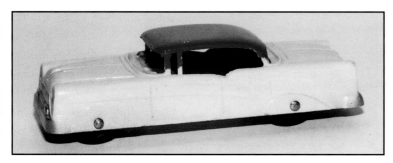

Oldsmobile 98
4", 1955, skirted fenders, rare version
$40.00/$45.00/$50.00

1955 Oldsmobile 98
4", 1955 – 1960, open fenders
$30.00/$35.00/$40.00

1959 Oldsmobile 88 Convertible
6", 1960 – 1968
$20.00/$30.00/$40.00

1956 Packard
4-door, 6", 1956 – 1959
no tow hook model
$30.00/$40.00/$50.00

1956 Packard
4-door, 6", 1956 – 1959
tow hook model
$35.00/$45.00/$55.00

1956 Packard
4-door, 6", rare
Note: Detailed bottom
$65.00/$75.00/$85.00

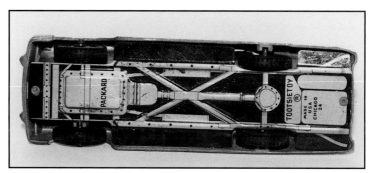

1950 Plymouth Sedan
4-door, 3", 1951 – 1954
$20.00/$25.00/$30.00

1957 Plymouth
2-door, 3", 1959 – 1969
$15.00/$20.00/$25.00

1950 Pontiac Sedan
4", 1950 – 1954
$30.00/$35.00/$40.00

1950 Pontiac Sedan
4", 1950 – 1954, rare two-tone
$35.00/$40.00/$45.00

1950 Pontiac Fire Chief
4", 1950 – 1954
$40.00/$50.00/$60.00

1959 Pontiac Sedan
4", 1961 – 1969
$20.00/$25.00/$30.00

1956 Porsche Roadster
5", 1959 – 1964
$30.00/$40.00/$50.00

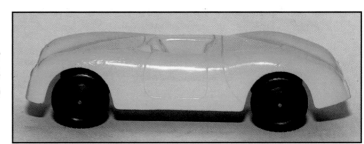

1960 Rambler Wagon
4", 1961 – 1963, semi-rare
$20.00/$25.00/$30.00

1947 Studebaker
3", 1949
$70.00/$80.00/$90.00

1960 Studebaker Lark Convertible
3", 1960 – 1964
$20.00/$25.00/$30.00

1955 Thunderbird Coupe
4", 1955 – 1967
$25.00/$30.00/$35.00

1955 Thunderbird Coupe
3", 1955 – 1960
$20.00/$25.00/$30.00

1956, Triumph TR3 Roadster
3", 1963 – 1969
$15.00/$20.00/$25.00

1956 Triumph TR3 Roadster
3", 1964, plastic
Colors: Red, blue, green
$10.00/$15.00/$20.00

1960 VW Bug
3", 1960 – 1964
$15.00/$20.00/$25.00

1960 VW Bug
5", 1960 – 1964, rare
$30.00/$40.00/$50.00

1947 Jeepster
3", 1949 – 1952
$25.00/$30.00/$35.00

1950 CJ3 Civilian Jeep
2½", 1952 – 1955, 1958 – 1961
$20.00/$25.00/$30.00

1947 CJ3 Civilian Jeep
4"
1947 – 1954, rubber tires
1955 – 1969, plastic tires
$20.00/$25.00/$30.00

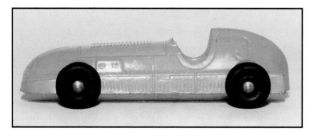

1949 Racer
3", 1949 – 1954
$25.00/$30.00/$35.00

1949 Civilian Jeep
6", sold separate and in sets
$20.00/$30.00/$40.00

1956 CJ5 Jeep
5", 1956 – 1959, windshield up
$25.00/$30.00/$35.00

1956 CJ5 Jeep
5", 1961, windshield down
$30.00/$35.00/$40.00

1956 CJ5 Jeep
6", 1961, rare, with snowplow
$40.00/$45.00/$50.00

1956 CJ5 Jeep
6", 1961, rare
windshield down with snowplow
$45.00/$50.00/$55.00

Buses, Dozers, and Miscellaneous Tootsietoys (HO, Midget, and Classic Series)

Tootsietoy buses came in all sizes and shapes produced both before and after the war. The Jumbo Series TransAmerica is the rarest bus to find for your collection. It came in red and silver and blue and silver. The Jumbo buses also came with a black tinplate bottom, which was often lost.

The small Midget Series Tootsietoys were produced from 1936 to 1941. They were packaged in two different ways — a small petitioned box and a small flat box with cutouts for the toys. The small game pieces and party favor assortments weren't considered midgets. Examples of the many Cracker Jack pieces and game pieces are pictured in this chapter.

The Classic Series was introduced in the early 1960s and had a short production until 1965. The 1921 Mack Dump was sold separately and is really rare. Earlier models had gold plastic spoke-like wheels, but the Model A has solid plastic black wheels or tires.

The rare little four-inch pull wagon with its wire looped handle was sold in set No. 4615 in 1947. This toy is extremely scarce today. All of the pieces I have seen have been painted red with silver trim on the front of the toy.

The small little road signs and toy badges were items from different bagged toys and boxed sets.

The Corvair, Cadillac convertible, and Rambler wagon were all made by Lone Star, a company in England that produced the Matchbox looking models. The Ford Sunliner completes this series of vehicles.

In 1932 Tootsietoy came out with a series called the Funnies Series which had a limited production run because at that time, they were not as popular as other models. The Funnies Series models were Andy Gump, Uncle Walt, Smitty, Moon Mullins, KO Ice, and Uncle Willie. These pieces, if found at shows, will be priced at approximately $350.00 – $500.00. Do you know what a good return on the original boxed set No. 5091 containing all six pieces would bring? Remember, the set retailed for only $1.00 in 1932 catalogs.

If I missed anything other than the doll furniture that I mentioned in the introduction, please feel free to let me know. The new chapter now contains all Tractors and all HO series rare mini vans.

No. 4651 Fageol Bus
1927 – 1933
$55.00/$75.00/$95.00

No. 4654 Farm Tractor
1927 – 1932, no hook
$80.00/$120.00/$160.00

No. 4654 Farm Tractor
1927 – 1932, with hook
$80.00/$120.00/$160.00

No. 4680 Overland Bus
1929 – 1933, separate grill
$85.00/$120.00/$155.00

Box Trailer Roadscraper Set
1928 – 1932
$150.00/$200.00/$250.00

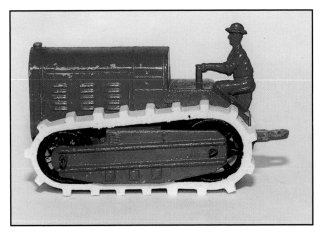

No. 4646 Caterpillar Tractor
1931 – 1939
$40.00/$70.00/$100.00

No. 4648 Steamroller
1931 – 1934, rare
$120.00/$170.00/$220.00

No. 5101X Andy Gump
 1932 – 1933
$350.00 – 500.00

No. 5102X Uncle Walt
1932 – 1933
$350.00 – 500.00

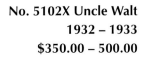

No. 5103X Smitty
1932 – 1933
$375.00 – 600.00

No. 5104X Moon Mullins
1932 – 1933
$350.00 – 500.00

No. 5106X Uncle Willie
1932 – 1933
$350.00 – 500.00

No. 5105X KO Ice
1932 – 1933
$350.00 – 500.00

No. 4654 Army Tractor
1931 – 1932, rare
Note: Ammo box
$100.00/$150.00/$200.00

No. 1045 Greyhound Bus
1937 – 1941
$60.00/$75.00/$90.00

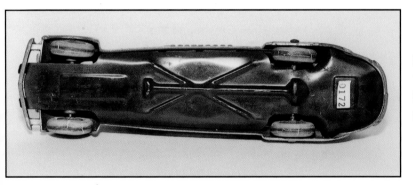

No. 1045 Greyhound Bus
1937 – 1941
Note: Tin bottom
$75.00/$90.00/$105.00

No. 1045 Greyhound Bus
1942 – 1946, rubber tires
$45.00/$60.00/$75.00

No. 1026 Greyhound Bus
1937 – 1939, solid color
$60.00/$75.00/$90.00

No. 1026 Greyhound Bus
1937 – 1939
Note: Tin bottom
$75.00/$90.00/$105.00

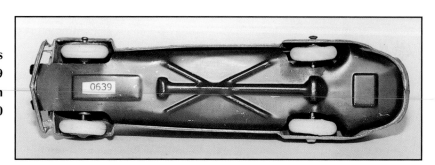

No. 1026 Greyhound Bus
1937 – 1939, wood wheels
$45.00/$60.00/$75.00

No. 3571 GMC Bus
1948 – 1955
$45.00/$60.00/$75.00

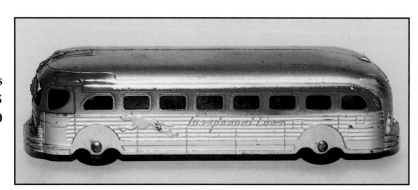

1949 Twin Coach Bus
3", 1949 – 1950
$35.00/$45.00/$55.00

1955 GMC Scenicruiser
7", 1955 – 1969
plastic tires later models
$35.00/$45.00/$55.00

No. 1910 Cat Bulldozer
4¼", 1956 – 1967
Sold without blade also
$40.00/$50.00/$60.00

1956 No. 3710 Cat Scraper
5½", 1956–1959, metal blade
$45.00/$55.00/$65.00

1956 No. 3710 Cat Scraper
5½", 1960 – 1967, plastic blade
$40.00/$50.00/$60.00

"TRANSAMERICA Bus"
sets only 1941, rare
Note: With and without tin bottom
$175.00/$200.00/$225.00

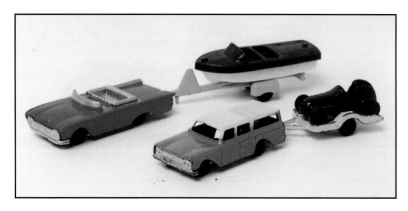

HO Series Ford and Rambler
1960s
$20.00/$30.00/$40.00

HO Series Cadillac
1960s
$20.00/$30.00/$40.00

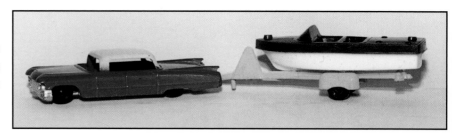

HO Series No. 2470 Dump Truck
1960s
$25.00/$35.00/$45.00

HO Series No. 2485 Tow Truck
1960s
$25.00/$35.00/$45.00

HO Series No. 2490 School Bus
1960s, rare
$35.00/$45.00/$55.00

HO Series No. 2465 Metro Milk and U. S. Mail
1960s
$55.00/$65.00/$75.00

HO Series No. 2465 Metro Railway Express
1960s
$45.00/$55.00/$65.00

Pull Wagon with handle
4", 1947, rare
Note: Handle should be straight
$75.00/$100.00/$125.00

HO Series No. 2465 Metro
Dry Cleaners Parcel Service
1960s
$55.00/$65.00/$75.00

Midget Series
Stake truck, Limo, Doodlebug,
Railcar, Racer, Fire truck
2", 1935 – 1941
$10.00/$15.00/$20.00

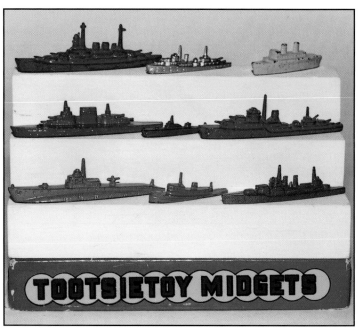

Midget Series
Cannon, Tank, Armored Car,
Tow truck, Camelback van
1" – 2", 1935 – 1941
$10.00/$15.00/$20.00

Midget Series
Assorted Ships
1" – 2", 1935 – 1941
$10.00/$15.00/$20.00

Midget Series
Single engine plane, St.
Louis, Bomber, Atlantic Clipper
1" – 2", 1935 – 1941
$10.00/$15.00/$20.00

Assorted Road Signs
from bagged toys & boxed sets
$6.00/$8.00/$10.00

**Classic Series
1907 Stanley Steamer
1960 – 1965
$25.00/$30.00/$35.00**

**Classic Series
1912 Ford Model T
1960 – 1965
$25.00/$30.00/$35.00**

**Classic Series
1929 Ford Model A
1960 – 1965
$25.00/$30.00/$35.00**

**Classic Series
1919 Stutz Bearcat
1960 – 1965
$25.00/$30.00/$35.00**

Classic Series
1906 Cadillac
1960 – 1965
$30.00/$35.00/$40.00

Classic Series
1922 Mack Dump
1960 only, rare
$40.00/$50.00/$60.00

Classic Series
1912 Ford Model T
Gold promo?, rare
$35.00/$40.00/$45.00

Classic Series
1906 Cadillac
Gold promo?, rare
$35.00/$40.00/$45.00

1960 Corvair
4", 1960 – 1961, English made
$55.00/$65.00/$75.00

1960 Rambler
4", 1960 – 1961, English made
$55.00/$65.00/$75.00

1960 Cadillac
4½", 1960 – 1961, English made
$65.00/$75.00/$85.00

Ford Sunliner
4¼", 1960 – 1961, English made
Rarest in series
$75.00/$85.00/$95.00

No. 1011 Massey Tractor
1941 catalog only, rare in red or green
$175.00/$200.00/$250.00

No. 289 Ford Tractor
1952 – 1955
Less detailed motor, spoked front tires
$80.00/$90.00/$100.00

Ford Tractor
1956 – 1969
detailed motor, no spoked front tires
$75.00/$85.00/$95.00

No. 2810 Tractor & Harrow
Less detailed motor
$90.00/$100.00/$110.00

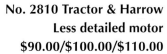

No. 3900 Tractor & Scoop
1959, detailed motor
$100.00/$110.00/$120.00

Ford Tractor
1960s, cast seat and steering wheel
$70.00/$80.00/$90.00

Ford Tractor
1960s, cast seat and steering wheel with scoop
$90.00/$100.00/$110.00

Ford Tractor & Scoop
1960s, separate seat and steering wheel
$100.00/$110.00/$120.00

No. 290 Tractor with/Shovel and Wagon
1952 – 1954, rare
$150.00/$175.00/$200.00

Fire Chief Badges
Tootsietoy: $55.00/$65.00/$75.00
Junior: $20.00/$25.00/$30.00

Assorted Winged Badges
from various sets
Pilot, Co-pilot, and Stewardess
$25.00/$35.00/$45.00

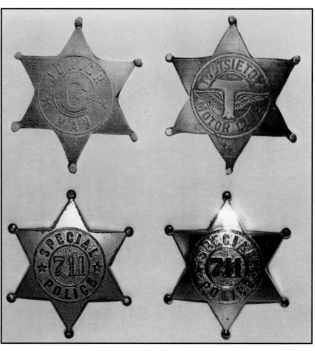

Assorted Star Badges
G-Man, Tootsietoy Motor Club
$50.00/$75.00/$100.00
Special 711 Police
$20.00/$25.00/$30.00

Eagle on top badges
G-Man, Deputy, Sunkist
$25.00/$30.00/$35.00

Davy Crockett Badge
1952?, rare
$55.00/$65.00/$75.00

Gas Pump Island
1963 – 1966, plastic
$20.00/$25.00/$30.00

Gas Pump Island
5½", 1960s
metal, in sets only
$40.00/$50.00/$60.00

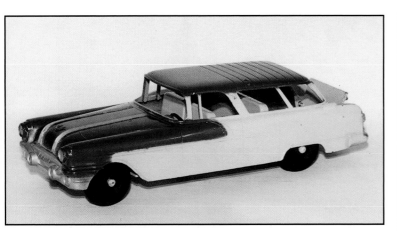

No. 895 Pontiac Safari Wagon
7", 1956 – 1958
$100.00/$175.00/$250.00

No. 995 Mercedes Benz 300 SL
7", 1956 – 1958
$125.00/$200.00/$275.00

No. 4656 Coupe in Garage
1931 – 1932
$100.00/$125.00/$150.00

No. 4657 Sedan in Garage
1931 – 1932
$100.00/$125.00/$150.00

No. 4658 Insurance Patrol in Garage
1931 – 1932
$110.00/$135.00/$160.00

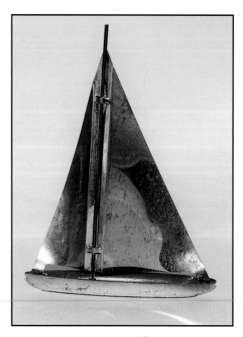

No. 718 Sailboat
5" x 6½", 1937 only, rare
$75.00/$100.00/$125.00

No. 2005 Hot Rod
Terrible Tommy, 1966
$75.00/$100.00/$125.00

No. 2010 M. G. Roadster
Pony-tailed Terry, 1966
$75.00/$100.00/$125.00

No. 2015 M. G. Roadster
Tubby Teddy, 1966
$75.00/$100.00/$125.00

No. 2457 Hot Rod
Hot Rod Herman, 1965
$75.00/$100.00/$125.00

No. 2457 Lancia Racer
Hot Rod Herman, 1965
$75.00/$100.00/$125.00

No. 2457 Ferrari Racer
Hot Rod Herman, 1965
$75.00/$100.00/$125.00
add $25.00 for MOC toy

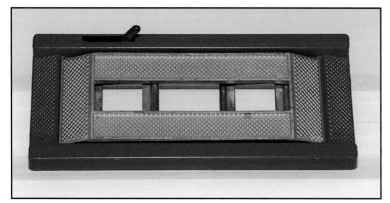

Auto Car Lift
1960s, in sets only
$30.00/$35.00/$40.00

Harrow Plow and Manure Wagon
Used in farm sets only
$40.00/$50.00/$60.00

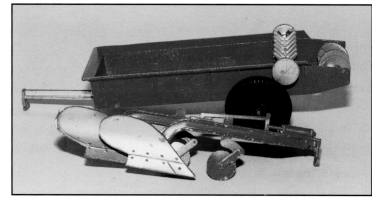

No. 4341 Telephone
1925
$55.00/$65.00/$75.00

No. 122 Telephone
1937, assorted colors
$25.00/$35.00/$45.00

General Motors Series
1927 – 1933

This group of toy cars and screen-sided vans had six basic body styles which were interchangeable on four styles of chassis. The combinations made up 24 different models each having its own catalog number.

The six different bodies styles were Coupe, Roadster, Brougham, Sedan, Touring Car Sedan, and a detailed Screenside Delivery Van. The chassis types were the Chevrolet, Buick, Oldsmobile, Cadillac, and later no-name types.

In the series, late in 1933, a nameless model was made of each body type. The radiator grills were without any raised lettering like other models in the series. These vehicles had the optional white rubber tires on a small cast rim instead of the disc wheel tire combination. Wheels of this type were later used on the 1934 Ford series 3" toys and various Mack Army 3" models.

Gold painted disc wheels appeared on 1927 and 1928 models. Wheels were painted black from 1929 through 1933, the only exception being some later 1932 and 1933 pieces that had the small white rubber tires on cast rims.

I tend to agree with my fellow authors and collector friends that the Buicks are the most common in the series and the nameless would be more difficult to obtain for a complete collection.

The hardest and last body type for my own collection was the open Tourer with its top up. The nicely colored photos in this section will better illustrate to you some of the many color schemes used on this great series of automobiles and panel delivery vans.

Examples in this series can be purchased at local toy shows from $45.00 to way over $100.00 depending on condition of the toy and your state or locale. Many of these ten cent toys are still available to the collector. Have fun collecting this complete series with its nicely colored toys. These will make a fine addition to anyone's Tootsietoy collection.

Examples in the photos that follow are all original toys that have not been restored.

Photo showing various grill fronts

Catalog Numbers

No. 6001	Buick Roadster	$65.00/$80.00/$95.00
No. 6002	Buick Coupe	$65.00/$80.00/$95.00
No. 6003	Buick Brougham	$70.00/$85.00/$100.00
No. 6004	Buick Sedan	$70.00/$85.00/$100.00
No. 6005	Buick Touring (closed)	$75.00/$100.00/$125.00
No. 6101	Cadillac Roadster	$80.00/$110.00/$135.00
No. 6102	Cadillac Coupe	$75.00/$100.00/$125.00
No. 6103	Cadillac Brougham	$80.00/$110.00/$135.00
No. 6104	Cadillac Sedan	$80.00/$110.00/$135.00
No. 6105	Cadillac Touring (closed)	$90.00/$115.00/$140.00
No. 6201	Chevrolet Roadster	$80.00/$110.00/$135.00
No. 6202	Chevrolet Coupe	$75.00/$100.00/$125.00
No. 6203	Chevrolet Brougham	$85.00/$110.00/$135.00
No. 6204	Chevrolet Sedan	$75.00/$100.00/$125.00
No. 6205	Chevrolet Touring (closed)	$90.00/$115.00/$140.00
No. 6301	Oldsmobile Roadster	$65.00/$80.00/$95.00
No. 6302	Oldsmobile Coupe	$65.00/$80.00/$95.00
No. 6303	Oldsmobile Brougham	$70.00/$85.00/$100.00
No. 6304	Oldsmobile Sedan	$70.00/$85.00/$100.00
No. 6305	Oldsmobile Touring (closed)	$90.00/$115.00/$140.00
No. 6-01	Roadster	$90.00/$120.00/$145.00
No. 6-02	Coupe	$90.00/$120.00/$145.00
No. 6-03	Brougham	$90.00/$120.00/$145.00
No. 6-04	Sedan	$90.00/$120.00/$145.00
No. 6-05	Touring (closed)	$100.00/$125.00/$150.00
No. 6006	Buick Delivery Van	$75.00/$100.00/$125.00
No. 6106	Cadillac Delivery Van	$80.00/$110.00/$135.00
No. 6206	Chevrolet Delivery Van	$80.00/$110.00/$135.00
No. 6306	Oldsmobile Delivery Van	$75.00/$100.00/$125.00
No. 6-06	No Name Delivery Van	$100.00/$125.00/$150.00

Roadster

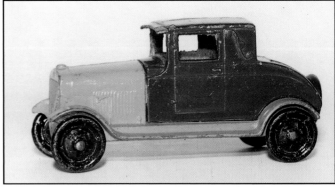

Coupe

Sedan

Brougham

Tourer

Delivery Van

Tootsietoy Grahams
1933 – 1939

Dowst Manufacturing Company introduced the Graham series in its new line-up for 1933. It included the Grahams in all their new colors and great detail with nickel-plated shiny grill fronts. The two-piece bodies of basically eight styles were mounted on several different chassis designs.

The body types were Coupe, Sedan, Wrecker, Ambulance, Roadster, Town Car, Dairy Van, and the limited production Commercial Tire Van.

There are two basic methods in which the Grahams were put together. One is the "BILD-A-CAR" sets by which divided axles, held by small clips in the center, connected the body to the chassis. The other type has a long nail passing through the wheel centers, going through the body lower loops, and being crimped on the passenger side of the toy, thus locking the body to the chassis.

Several actual Graham models never really existed in any of their catalogs. These included the Town Car without spare tire, Panel Vans with side spares, Station Wagon, and a Mail Truck Van. In the event you may encounter one of these odd balls, it was probably the result of some chopper or child's father trying to put together a one-of-a-kind toy for his child. There are, however, many minor variations of castings including body, chassis, grills, and wheels. It is almost impossible to date or pinpoint the exact years.

The convertible Coupes and Sedans were merely two-tone cars with a painted roof. A light khaki paint was applied to the roof to simulate the convertible top's being up on the toy. These models have their own catalog numbers as well.

In 1937 the Commercial Tire Van replaced the Roadster in boxed set No. 5360 BUILD-A-CAR set or BILD-A-CAR as spelled in Tootsietoy catalogs. The Commercial Tire Van carries the high price tag of $200.00 or more if you are lucky to find a nice example of this toy for sale.

Endless color combinations can be found in the BILD-A-CAR sets, TAXI boxed sets, and on individually packaged Grahams. There are over 100 different color combinations in all for the eight body types.

Happy collecting and good luck hunting these rascals down. Examples of body types with their catalog number will follow. Most of the toys pictured are original with a couple restored ones painted their original color schemes with new tires added.

Graham Sedan
Taxi Set
$100.00 – 125.00

Graham Coupe
BILD-A-CAR Set
$100.00 – 125.00

No. 0511 Graham 5 Wheel Roadster
$135.00 – 165.00 mint

No. 0512 Graham 5 Wheel Coupe
$135.00 – 165.00 mint

No. 0513 Graham 5 Wheel Sedan
$135.00 – 165.00 mint

No. 0514 Graham 5 Wheel Convertible Coupe
$135.00 – 165.00 mint

No. 0515 Graham 5 Wheel Convertible Sedan
$135.00 – 165.00

No. 0516 Graham 5 Wheel Town Car
$140.00 – 170.00

No. 0611 Graham 6 Wheel Roadster
$160.00 – 190.00

No. 0612 Graham 6 Wheel Coupe
$135.00 – 165.00 mint

No. 0613 Graham 6 Wheel Seden
$135.00 – 165.00 mint

No. 0614 Graham 6 Wheel Convertible Coupe
$140.00 – 170.00 mint

No. 0615 Graham 6 Wheel Convertible Sedan
$135.00 – 165.00 mint

No. 0616 Graham 6 Wheel Town Car
$140.00 – 170.00 mint

No. 0809 Graham Civilian Ambulance
$100.00/$125.00/$150.00

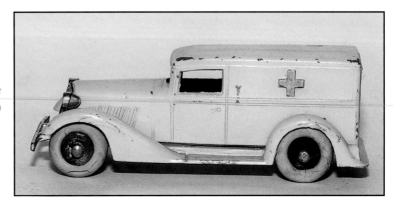

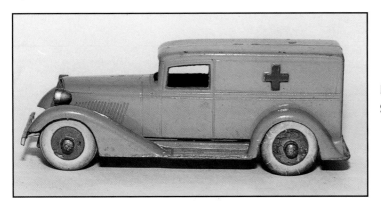

No. 0809 Graham Army Ambulance
$100.00/$125.00/$150.00

No. 0809 Graham Army Ambulance
Camouflaged, white tires
$100.00/$135.00/$160.00

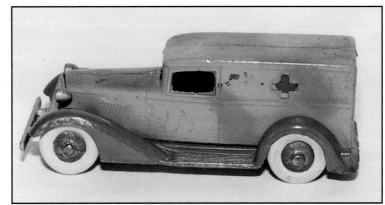

No. 0809 Graham Army Ambulance
Camouflaged, black tires, rare
$125.00/$150.00/$200.00

No. 0808 Graham Dairy Van
$130.00/$160.00/$185.00

No Number, Commercial Tire Van
Sets only
$150.00/$175.00/$240.00

No. 0806 Graham Wrecker
$100.00/$125.00/$150.00

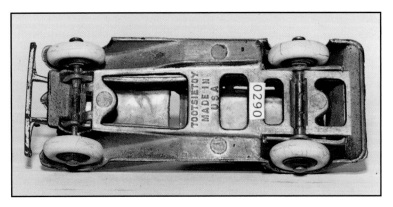

Graham BILD-A-CAR
Bottom view
Note: Small sleeves center of axles

Graham 4 Wheel Roadster
Later sets only
Note: Has solid floor under rumble seat
No price available

Graham Sedan
Dealer Promo, 1933, rare
Note: Special paint and red hubs
No price available

Made in Mexico
"tutsitoys"

Several Tootsietoy discontinued dies from the late fifties were used to produce many models for the Mexican market. It was an arrangement the Strombecker Corporation made with Mexico.

Almost all the toys examples were still marked TOOTSIETOY MADE IN USA. The blister package or box with its Spanish language on the front made it easy to identify. The caption "MADE IN MEXICO" was usually located on all the toy packaging at the bottom of blister pack or box.

Mexican "tutsitoys" can be found in 3", 4", 6" toys and Jam Pacs with smaller assorted vehicles. They have primitive black soft rubber tires without the Tootsietoy logo at the edge of the tires sidewall. They also lacked the silver painted trim on grill fronts and bumpers on many earlier American examples of the same toys.

Mexican "tutsitoys" were still in production well into the late eighties. Occasionally a few crop up at local toy shows still in their original packaging. Be on the lookout for the yellow and red packaging colors. Its an eye catcher for sure. I regret that I do not have more examples to show you. Good luck hunting these jewels down.

Mexican Jam Pac
Six vehicles, 1960s
No price available

RC 180 PEMEX Oil Tanker
Mexico
No price available

Three-piece Set
AUXILIO VIAL Tow Truck, 3", Mack
PEMEX Oil Tanker
Mexico
No price available

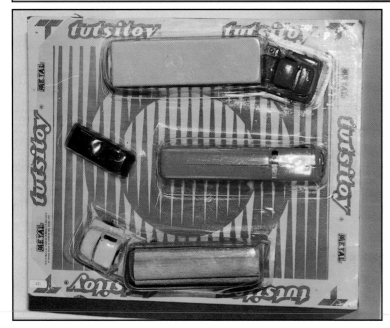

Four-piece Set
Jaguar, Greyhound Bus
Utility Truck, AUTO EXPRESS Van
3", Mexico
No price available

RC 180 Utility Semi
Mexico
No price available

Ford PEMEX Oil
6", Mexico
No price available

Mack Tow Truck
Mexico
No price available

Military Items

Tootsietoy, like its competitors of the early 1930s and 1950s, produced some very nice detailed toys. The No. 4643 Mack Gun Truck and No. 4644 Searchlight Truck were produced with different wheel types and paint schemes. The small black die-steel wheels are the most common type. Miniature white rubber tires mounted on separate rims would be the rarest. The same type of wheel was also used on the 1934 Ford 3" cars. The last type is a solid white rubber tire produced from 1935 until around 1941.

The many military vehicle types can be found in solid colors or the very nice camouflaged paint schemes. Post-war production brought back many familiar pieces from the pre-war years. Different tires were the most obvious changes. Tires were replaced with a black rubber tire for better wear.

In the 1950s and early 1960s many of the pieces were sold in boxed sets, blister packages, and separately boxed toys. Several sets contained a plastic soldier or two along with other military vehicles. Like all original boxed sets, be prepared to pay a lot more than the actual values listed for individual pieces in my guide. Very few examples exist and they are rarely for sale in today's toy market.

The Army Jeeps of all three sizes are quite easy to purchase for your collection. The only real exception is the CJ5 Military Jeep with its yellow snow plow. Several items are on the rare list like the Army Radar Trailer, 155mm Howitzer Tank, and the 1955 RC 180 Army or Navy Rocket Launcher and Rocket Trucks. Separate models are located hereafter.

No. 4642 Long Range Cannon
1931 – 1940
$25.00/$30.00/$35.00

No. 4662 Mortar Cannon
1933 only, very rare
orange and gray colors
$55.00/$65.00/$75.00

No. 4642 Long Range Cannon
1941 – 1942, 1946
rubber tires
$20.00/$25.00/$30.00

No. 4643 Mack Anti-Aircraft Gun
1931, metal wheels
$45.00/$55.00/$65.00

No. 4643 Mack Anti-Aircraft Gun
1933, tires on metal hubs
$45.00/$55.00/$65.00

No. 4643 Mack Anti-Aircraft Gun
1940, white tires, camouflaged
$45.00/$55.00/$65.00

No. 4644 Mack Searchlight
1931, metal wheels
$50.00/$60.00/$70.00

No. 4644 Mack Searchlight
1933, tires on hubs
$50.00/$60.00/$70.00

No. 4644 Mack Searchlight
1940, white tires, camouflaged
$50.00/$60.00/$70.00

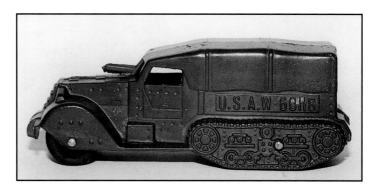

Army Half Track
1941, 1960s
$30.00/$35.00/$40.00

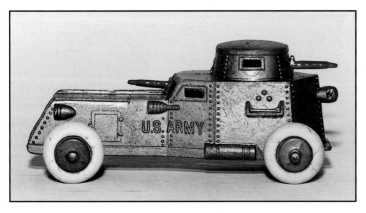

No. 4635 Armored Car
1938
$45.00/$55.00/$65.00

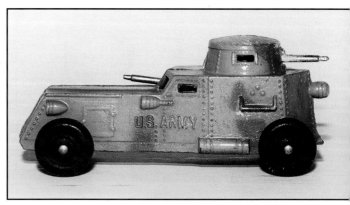

No. 4635 Armored Car
1946 – 1948, camouflaged
$40.00/$45.00/$50.00

No. 4635 Armored Car
1942 – 1946
$35.00/$40.00/$45.00

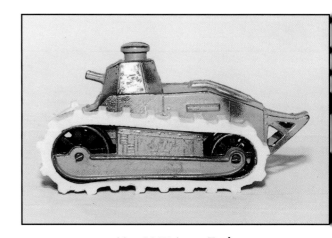

No. 4647 Army Tank
Renault, 1931 – 1941
$50.00/$60.00/$70.00

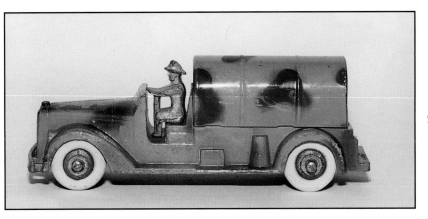

No. 4634 Army Supply Truck
1931
$65.00/$75.00/$85.00

CJ3 1950 Army Jeep
2½", 1955
Note: No cast steering wheel on dashboard
$20.00/$25.00/$30.00

CJ3 1950 Army Jeep
2½", 1958, rubber and plastic tires
$15.00/$20.00/$25.00

CJ3 1947 Army Jeep
4", 1947 – 1965
All tires and axle types
$25.00/$30.00/$35.00

Chevy Ambulance
4", 1950
$30.00/$35.00/$40.00

Ford F700 Army Stake
6", 1956, rare
$65.00/$75.00/$85.00

Ford F700 Army Radar
6", 1956, metal screen
$55.00/$65.00/$75.00

Ford F700 Army Radar
6", 1956, plastic screen
$45.00/$55.00/$65.00

Ford F700 Army Anti-Aircraft Gun
6", 1956, metal guns
$55.00/$65.00/$75.00

Ford F700 Army Anti-Aircraft Gun
6", 1956, plastic guns
$40.00/$50.00/$60.00

Ford F700 Searchlight Gun
6", 1956
$65.00/$75.00/$85.00

Four Wheel Cannon
4", 1950s
$20.00/$25.00/$30.00

Army Tank
1958 – 1960
$20.00/$25.00/$30.00

Army Searchlight Trailer
3", 1950, semi-rare
$35.00/$40.00/$45.00

Six Wheel Army Cannon
4", 1950, solid frame
$25.00/$30.00/$35.00

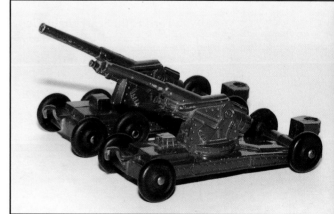

Four Wheel Army Cannon
4", 1950, large barrel, four tires
$30.00/$35.00/$40.00

Army Radar Trailer
3", 1959 – 1960, rare
$65.00/$75.00/$85.00

155m Howitzer Tank
5", 1958 – 1960
$80.00/$100.00/$120.00

Oldsmobile Staff Car
4", 1958 – 1960
$40.00/$45.00/$50.00

Thunderbird Staff Car
4", 1958 – 1960
$45.00/$50.00/$55.00

41 International Army Ambulance
4", 1949
$45.00/$50.00/$55.00

Modern Field Cannon
5", 1958 – 1965
$25.00/$30.00/$35.00

RC 180 Army Lowboy Trailer
8½", 1965, rare
$60.00/$75.00/$90.00

CJ5 Army Jeep
5", 1956, windshield up
$25.00/$30.00/$35.00

CJ5 Army Jeep
5", 1951, windshield down
$20.00/$25.00/$30.00

CJ5 Army Jeep with Snowplow
5½", 1961
$30.00/$40.00/$50.00

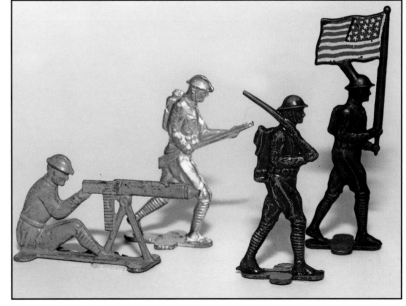

Tootsietoy Soldiers
1938, four types
$35.00/$45.00/$55.00

RC 180 Army Rocket Launcher
8½", 1958 – 1960
$120.00/$135.00/$150.00

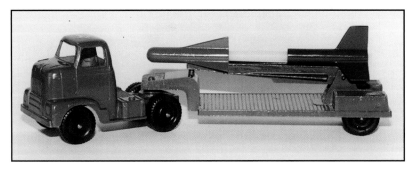

RC 180 Airforce Rocket Launcher
8", 1958 – 1960, rarest
$130.00/$145.00/$160.00

Army Jeep
6", 1950s, all tire types
$30.00/$35.00/$40.00

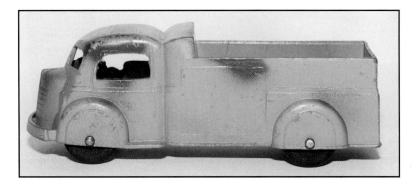

No. 1010 Army Box Van
4", camouflaged, years unknown
No price available

No. 4666 Army Caterpillar
camouflaged
No price available

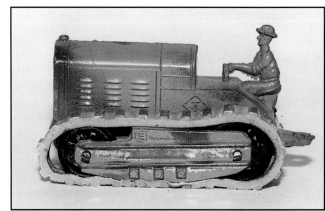

Packaged Toys and Boxed Sets

Packaged toys and boxed sets of Tootsietoys are very hard to obtain. The first type of packaging used was a small plastic or cellophane-like bag. The toy or toys were put in the bag and stapled at the top. A small hole was punched in the bag top so it could be hung on the various types of counter displays and free standing vertical display racks.

The next form of packaging was the most common blister pack. The toy or toys were placed on a colorful cardboard backing with a heavy plastic placed on top of the toy and heated, thus sealing the toy airtight. A small cardboard box with the toy clearly illustrated on the outside and a catalog number on the two end flaps of the box was the third type of packaging.

Boxed sets are probably the most popular with collectors of all the various packaging. As a rule, you could add 20% or more to the boxed set of pieces depending on condition of the box in which they were originally packaged.

I have included many examples of packaging and some boxed sets that I have in my collection along with examples from several friends who were kind enough to allow me to photograph them. All photos in this chapter are new items and not found in my previous book.

Happy collecting!

No. 5091 Tootsietoy Funnies Set
1932, 1933
No price available

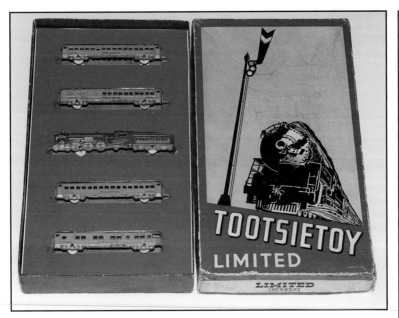

No. 5850 Passenger Limited Train Set
1940, 1941, 1942/1946
$240.00 – 400.00

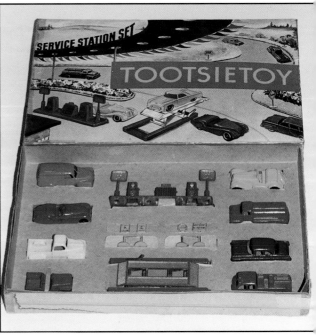

No. 4200 Service Station Set
1959, 1960
$250.00 – 400.00

No. 2415 Austin-Healy Kit
1961 only, rare
$125.00 – 175.00

No. 3111 1922 Mack Truck
1961 – 1962
$75.00 – 125.00

No. 2470 HO Dump Truck
1960 – 1962
$50.00 – 90.00

No. 3003 Classic Cadillac
1960 – 1962
$90.00 – 120.00

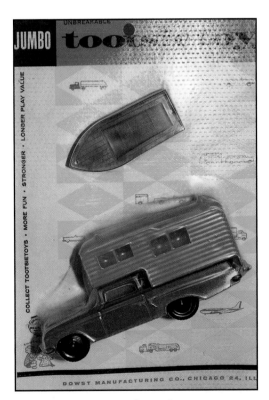

No. 2300 El Camino Camper
1961 – 1964
$100.00 – 135.00

No. 1686 Farm Set
1967, four piece
$60.00 – 90.00

No. 2926 U-Haul Moving Van
1964 – 1965
No price available

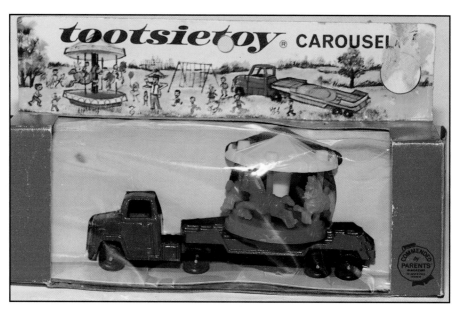

No. 1464 Carousel Truck
1968, rare
$50.00 – 100.00

No. 389 Tractor and Scoop
1960s
$125.00 – 165.00

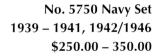

Number Unknown
1969 LTD U-Haul Set
1969 – 1970
$45.00 – 75.00

No. 5750 Navy Set
1939 – 1941, 1942/1946
$250.00 – 350.00

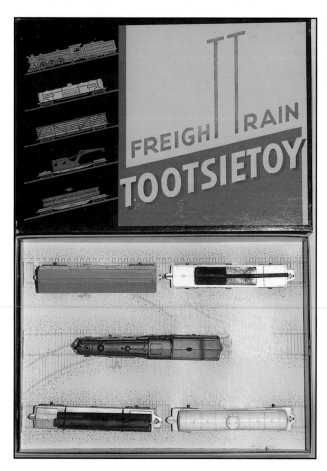

No. 5550 Freight Train Set
1939 – 1941, rare
Set shown 1941 with special insert
No price available

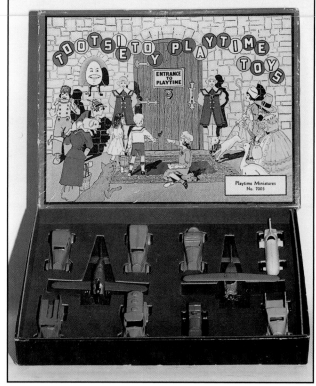

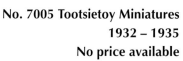

No. 7005 Tootsietoy Miniatures
1932 – 1935
No price available

No. 4626 Tootsietoy Limited Train
1929, 1931, 1932
No price available

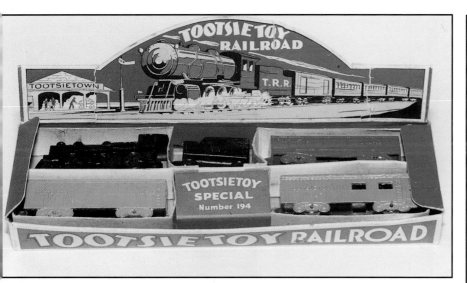

No.194 Freight Train Set
1934 – 1938
$175.00 – 350.00

No. 4660 Aero Dawn w/box
1929, 1931, 1932
$125.00 – 225.00

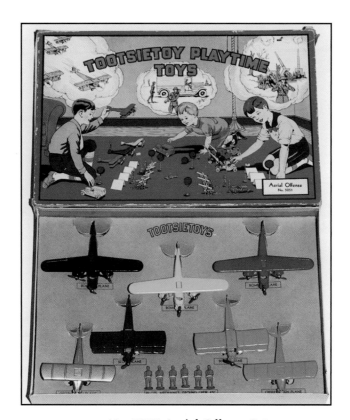

No. 5051 Aerial Offense Set
1931 – 1933
No price available

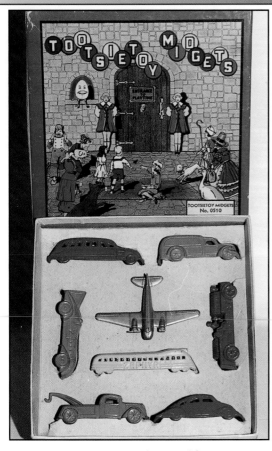

No. 0510 Tootsietoy Midgets
1936 – 1937
$200.00 – 250.00 mint

No. 200 Breakfast Set
1936
No. 201 Breakfast Set
1937 – 1941
$150.00 – 200.00 mint

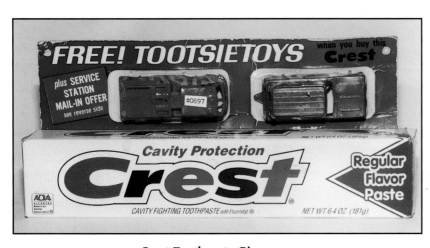

Crest Toothpaste Giveaway
1967, rare with cars attached
$50.00 – 80.00

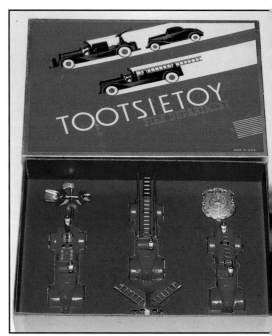

No. 411 Fire Dept. Set
1948 only, rarest fire set
$650.00 – 950.00 mint

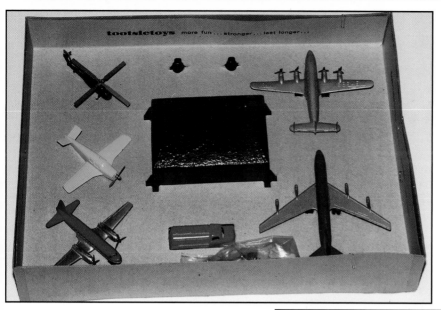

No. 4310 Pan American Airway Set
1958 – 1959, two variations
$550.00 – 750.00 mint

No. 4310 Pan American Airway Set (lid)

No. 7250 Toosietoy "MOTORS"
1953 – 1954 (box lid)

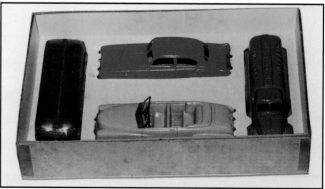

No. 7250 Tootsietoy "MOTORS" Set
1953 – 1954
$350.00 – 400.00

Ships

The Tootsietoy all-metal ships were introduced in the catalogs around 1940. There are ten different models. The ships are very fragile with their tiny cast guns, masts, flags, and airplanes on the No. 1036 Carrier and one plane on the No. 1035 Cruiser.

The all-metal ships actually came in two series of paint styles. Series one ships, which are much more common, are silver and red military and multicolor commercial vessels. The second series in 1941 and 1942 are gray and red, or the English type camouflage like No. 129 Tender pictured in this chapter.

Tootsietoy ships, like all other Tootsietoys, now are really getting hard to find in mint condition. I've seen some boxed sets of the war ships at shows priced more than double the price of the pieces themselves.

Ships of the 1970s are located in the chapter on Tootsietoys 1970 – 1979. The small 1" and 2" ships of the Midget Series are located in the Buses, Dozers, and Miscellaneous Tootsietoys chapter.

Collecting all ten ships in series one and series two paint schemes would be a challenge to any collector. I have been very fortunate to upgrade almost all my ships to mint examples.

The Tootsietoy all-metal ships were under valued in my revised value guide of 1993 and also other value guides. My new prices take into consideration the rarity of mint pieces and also take an average of show selling prices. Happy hunting!

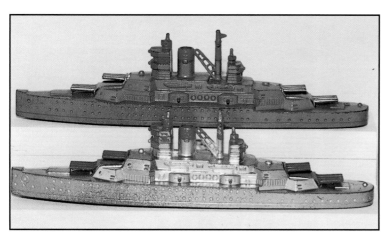

No. 1034 Battleship
$30.00/$35.00/40.00

No. 1035 Cruiser
$30.00/$35.00/$40.00

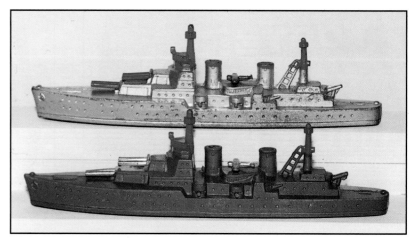

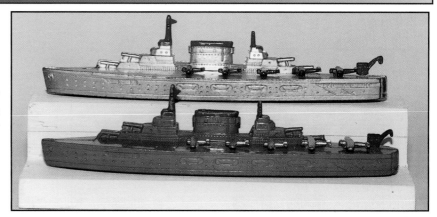

No. 1036 Carrier
$35.00/$40.00/$45.00

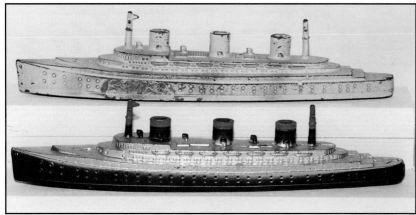

No. 1037 Transport
$30.00/$35.00/$40.00

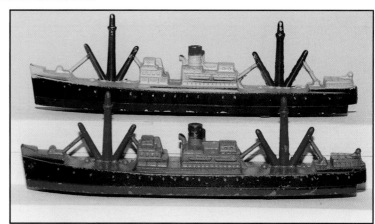

No. 1038 Freighter
$30.00/$35.00/$40.00

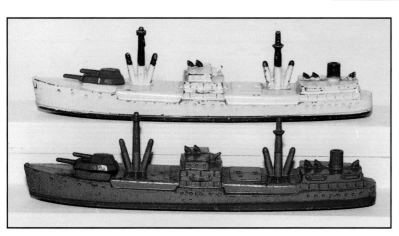

No. 1039 Tanker
$35.00/$40.00/$45.00

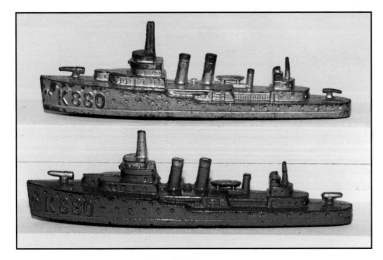

No. 127 Destroyer
$25.00/$30.00/$35.00

No. 128 Submarine
$25.00/$30.00/$35.00

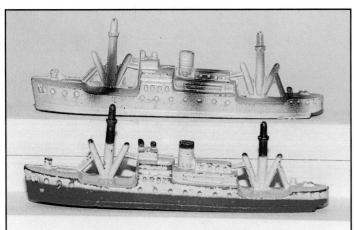

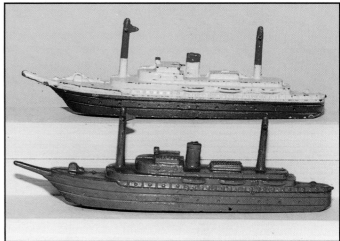

No. 129 Tender
English camouflage bottom
$25.00/$30.00/$35.00

No. 130 Yacht
$30.00/$35.00/$40.00

Trailers

Besides the Huber box trailer of the earlier years and the many cannons and military type trailers, others were produced to be pulled by vehicles — a 1937 Tootsietoy catalog pictures the No. 1043 small house trailer and No. 1044 Roamer trailer. The small camping or house trailer was always sold with a 1935 Ford 3" sedan that was the same color as the trailer. I've seen sets in red, blue, green, and silver (the most common). The No. 1044 Roamer trailer was designed for use with the La Salle Coupe and Sedan. It has a floor plate and sliding door through which it can be loaded. It was sold singly only in 1937, later only in set No. 180. The Roamer trailer by far is the rarest pre-war trailer.

Both 4" and 6" post-war trailers were usually packaged with a 6" car or pickup truck. Assorted trailers also help to make up several different camping sets. These include the different boat, house, horse, race car, and U-haul trailers. The restaurant and the 4½" Stake Trailer of 1963 are the hardest two trailers to obtain for your collection. A yellow Stake Trailer is pictured in this chapter, but missing its brown plastic stake-like tailgate. A packaged toy complete with Ford Econoline pickup truck is pictured in the Packaged Toys chapter.

Many other trailers are pictured in the 1970s chapter.

No. 1044 Roamer Trailer
1937 – 1939, rare
$200.00/$225.00/$250.00

Small House Trailer
1937 – 1939
Used with 35 Ford Sedan
$35.00/$45.00/$65.00

Horse Trailer
1961 – 1965, plastic top
$20.00/$25.00/$30.00

U-Haul Trailer
4", 1958 – 1961
$20.00/$25.00/$30.00

House Trailer
1960 – 1967, plastic top and door
$20.00/$30.00/$40.00

Boat Trailer
1959 – 1963
$20.00/$25.00/$30.00

Restaurant Trailer
1960 – 1961, 1963
Note: Has sign top
$40.00/$50.00/$60.00

Stake Trailer
1963, missing tailgate
$25.00/$35.00/$45.00

Race Car Trailer
1960 – 1961, 1963 – 1968
$20.00/$25.00/$30.00

Trains

The first Tootsietoy train, I believe, was the No. 4397 set produced in 1921. It consisted of an engine with a large smoke stack, tender, and two coaches finished in a beautiful silver-plate finish. I have never had a chance to see even a photo of this very rare train.

The 1932 catalog shows us many different freight and passenger trains. Many of the trains were produced in boxed sets, and separate pieces of train cars and engines were sold so a young child could construct a train with as many cars as he or she wanted. The No. 7002 Fast Freight Set consisted of a locomotive, tender, boxcar, gondola car, and a caboose, usually painted in bright colors. The No. 7002 set was repackaged and numbered No. 194 from 1932 to 1937. The Midnight Flyer Set No. 7001 was the passenger set of the same era. It consisted of a baggage car, pullman car, and an observation car at the end. They were painted a light pastel yellow, red, green, or blue. Engines and tenders of both trains above were always painted black. Set No. 7001 was also repackaged and renumbered as No. 193 from 1932 to 1937.

The year 1937 brought a totally new train, No. 196. This was a streamlined train consisting of three pieces in total. The train was a copy of the Union Pacific Flyer streamliner. I have this train in silver and also two-toned red and silver in my personal collection. I am told that a blue and silver version of this train exists also. The fall of 1937 brought still another new arrival to the already growing line of Tootsietoy trains — the Broadway Limited, a copy of that popular New York/Chicago train. The snub-nosed engine had Pennsylvania clearly marked on its tender in raised lettering. Engine and tender cars were cast in one piece for this new No. 188 set. To better distinguish the engine from others, it also carried number 5435 under the engine windows.

The years 1939 – 1941 brought the ever-popular No. 1086 Pennsylvania and No. 1076 Santa Fe Locomotives with nine different cars to build upon your engine and tender cars. All the cars were 5¼" in length. The only exceptions are the engine at 6" and the small caboose at 3¼" in length. Examples of engines and nine different cars are pictured in this chapter.

The Fast Freight set No. 186 issued around 1940 consisted of an engine, tender, and three cars. This set was sold in a long narrow colorful box. The Cracker Jack boxcar really makes this set highly collectible.

I now have No. 5420 Diesel Freight set pictured on page 132 of my third edition guide. This train is the rarest postwar train produced in limited quantities. Any comments or information about Tootsietoy trains or sets is most welcome. Thank you.

No. 4626 Passenger Train
Three piece
No. 4627 Freight Train
Three piece
1925, 1929, 1931, 1932
$100.00/$120.00/$140.00

No. 11 Passenger Train
1925, 5 piece, spoked wheels
$125.00/$150.00/$175.00

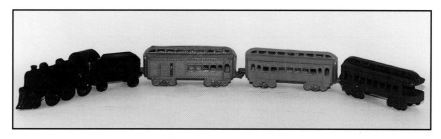

No. 7001 Passenger Train Set or later
No. 193 Set (same pieces new catalog numbers)
1932 – 1937
$125.00/$150.00/$175.00

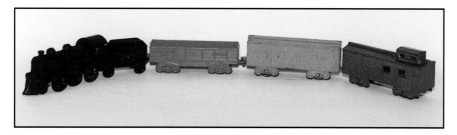

No. 7002 Freight Train Set or later
No. 194 Set (same pieces new catalog numbers)
1932 – 1937
$145.00/$170.00/$195.00

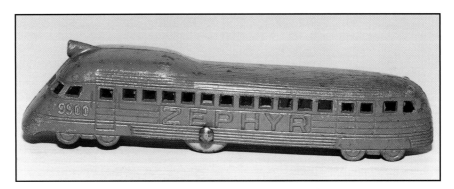

No. 117 Zephyr Railcar
1935, 4", rare
1935 – 1936
$100.00/$125.00/$150.00

No.196 Tootsietoy Flyer
1937 – 1941
Note: Sold separately and in many boxes sets
$135.00/$155.00/$175.00

No. 197 Tootsietoy Flyer
1937 – 1941, rare two-tone train
$150.00/$175.00/$200.00

No. 1076 Santa Fe
No. 1086 Pennsylvania
1939 – 1941, white tires
$25.00/$35.00/40.00 each

No. 1094 Oil Tank Car
$15.00/$20.00/25.00

No. 1093 Milk Tank Car
$20.00/$25.00/30.00

No. 1088 Refrigerator Car
$20.00/$25.00/30.00

No. 1089 Santa Fe Box Car
Black rubber tires
$20.00/$25.00/30.00

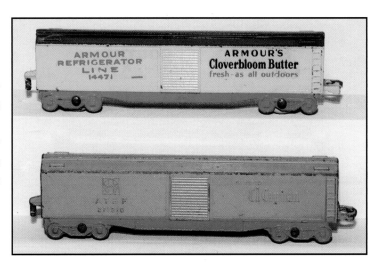

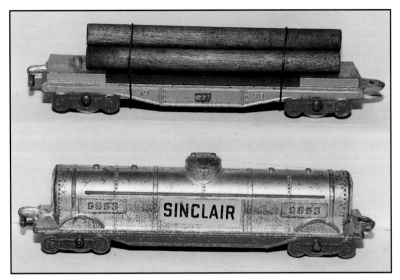

No. 1092 Log Car
$20.00/$25.00/$30.00

No. 1094
with stickers
$20.00/$25.00/$30.00

No. 1087 Wrecking Crane
$25.00/$30.00/$35.00

No. 1091 Stock Car
$15.00/$20.00/$25.00

No. 1089 Box Car
$20.00/$25.00/$30.00

No. 1090 Coal or Sand Car
$15.00/$20.00/$25.00

No. 1090 Coal Car
$15.00/$20.00/$25.00

No. 1095 Caboose
$20.00/$25.00/$30.00

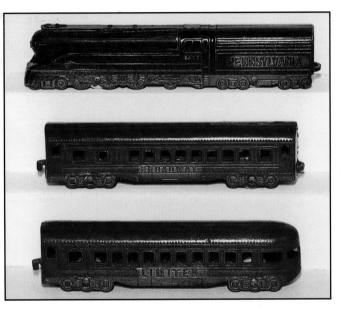

No. 188 Broadway
Limited Set, 1937
$150.00/$175.00/$200.00

No. 5851 Santa Fe or Pennsylvania
Limited Train Set, 1941
five-piece train, complete
$160.00/$200.00/$240.00

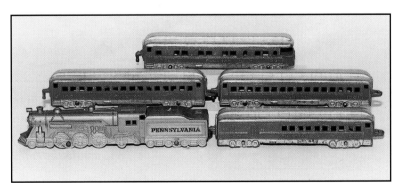

No. 186 Fast Freight Set
1940 – 1941, white rubber tires
$125.00/$150.00/$175.00

No. 186 Fast Freight Set
1942, 1946, 1949, 1950
black rubber tires
$120.00/$145.00/$170.00

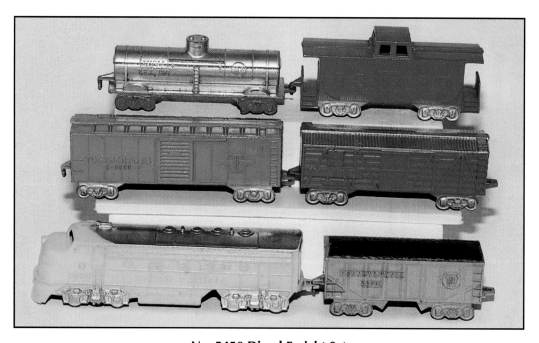

No. 5450 Diesel Freight Set
six-piece set, 26" in length
1950s, rarest postwar train set
$150.00/$200.00/$250.00

Trucks and Semis

Strombecker Corporation has produced thousands of trucks, vans, and tractor trailer combinations. The first truck appeared in the 1916 catalog No. 4610 Model T pickup with its tiny shiny gold spoked wheels. Spoked wheels were replaced by solid discs in 1924.

The Federal 3" Grocery, Market, Bakery, Laundry, Milk, and Florist vans appeared around 1924 and were last seen in the 1933 catalog. The Florist is the rarest of this group. In 1925 special Federals were produced for different department stores and businesses. Some names were BOGGS & BUHL, POMEROY'S, WATT & SHAND, J.C. PENNEY, and more. Sorry to say at this time I do not have these in my collection to photograph for you.

Ever-popular Mack 3" trucks were made in 1924 and first appeared without a chain drive at the rear and with an M on the hood for Mack. A Stake, Coal, and Oil were made both with and without chain drives cast by the rear axle. The Mail truck was produced between 1931 and 1933 and is the rarest of this short series.

The first set of two Mack trucks and trailers appeared around 1929. This was set No. 4670 containing an A & P Trailer and American Railway Express each with its own cab. The 1933 catalog showed the Mack Domaco Oil, Express, Moving Van, City Fuel, and Dairy, plus others. Examples with single axle trailers and single axle trailers with dual tires on one axle are pictured in this chapter with all the other great looking Macks. My favorite would be the No. 187 Transport with three No. 230 series automobiles that was only in the catalog for one year — 1941. Someday I would like to take a survey and see just how many of these No. 187 sets exist today.

Tootsietoy pre-war examples are harder to locate than most of the post-war trucks and trailers. The two most common 4" trucks were the Stake and Oil 1949 Fords. These trucks were in catalogs from 1949 to 1969, the longest production of any other Tootsietoy truck pictured in my value guide.

No. 4610 1914 Model T Pickup
3", 1916 – 1923, spoked wheels
$45.00/$55.00/$65.00

No. 4610 1914 Model T Pickup
3", 1924 – 1932
$40.00/$50.00/$60.00

No. 0801 Mack Stake Trailer
1933 – 1935, two-piece cab
$100.00/$125.00/$150.00

No. 0801 Mack Stake Trailer
1933 – 1941, one-piece cab
$75.00/$100.00/$125.00

No. 0802 Mack DOMACO Oil
1933 – 1935, two-piece cab
$100.00/$125.00/$150.00

No. 0802 Mack DOMACO Oil
1935 – 1939, one piece cab
$75.00/$100.00/$125.00

No. 0804 Mack Coal Truck
1933 – 1936, dual rear axle
$120.00/$140.00/$160.00

No. 0804 Mack Coal Truck
1937 – 1941, single rear axle, rare
Note: Cab one piece
$110.00/$130.00/$150.00

No. 0805 Mack Milk Truck
1933 – 1935, two-piece cab
$110.00/$130.00/$150.00

No. 0805 Mack Milk Truck
1937 – 1939, one-piece cab
$90.00/$120.00/$150.00

No. 0803 Mack Van Trailer
1933 – 1936
$110.00/$130.00/$150.00

No. 0192 Mack Milk Trailer Set
1933 – 1941, three-trailers
$160.00/$200.00/$240.00

No. 0191 Contractor Set
1933 – 1941
$125.00/$150.00/$175.00

No. 0190 Mack Transport
Shown with three 2" Buicks
$160.00/$190.00/$220.00

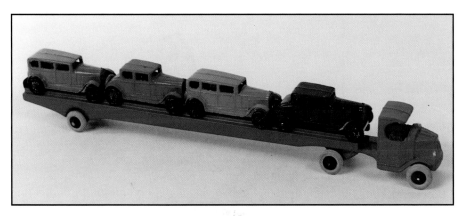

No. 00190X Mack Transport
Shown with four 3" Buicks, rare set
$390.00/$440.00/$475.00

No. 198 Auto Transport
Shown with three Ford cars
$180.00/$220.00/$260.00

No. 0810 Mack Wrigley's Gum
4", 1935 – 1941
$135.00/$155.00/$175.00

No. 0810 Mack Box Truck
Red in boxed sets only, rare
$145.00/$165.00/$185.00

No. 0807 Delivery Cycle
1933 – 1934
$120.00/$135.00/$150.00

No. 187 Mack Transport
1941 only, rare
$225.00/$250.00/$300.00

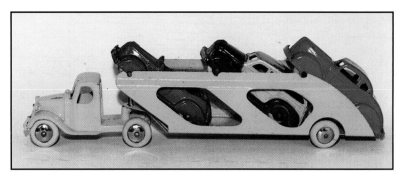

Federal Grocery Van
1924 – 1933
$110.00/$135.00/$160.00

Federal Laundry Van
1924 – 1933
$110.00/$135.00/$160.00

Federal Milk Van
1924 – 1933
$100.00/$125.00/$150.00

Federal Market Van
1924 – 1933
$110.00/$135.00/$160.00

Federal Bakery Van
1924 – 1933
$110.00/$135.00/$150.00

Federal Florist Van
1924 – 1933, rarest in series
$175.00/$200.00/$225.00

No. 4638 1925 Mack Stake
3", 1925 – 1928
$65.00/$75.00/$85.00

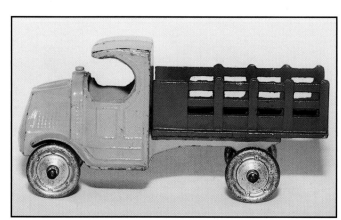

No. 4638 1928 Mack Stake
3", 1928 – 1923
$60.00/$70.00/$80.00

No. 4639 1925 Mack Coal
3", 1925 – 1928
$65.00/$75.00/$85.00

No. 4639 1928 Mack Coal
3", 1928 – 1923
$60.00/$70.00/$80.00

No. 4640 1925 Mack Oil
3", 1925 – 1928
$65.00/$75.00/$85.00

No. 4640 1928 Mack Oil
3", 1928 – 1933
$60.00/$70.00/$80.00

No. 4645 Mack Mail
3", 1931 – 1933
$75.00/$100.00/$125.00

No. 4652 Fire Hook & Ladder
3½", 1927 – 1933
$75.00/$100.00/$125.00

No. 4653 Fire Watertower Truck
3½", 1927 – 1933
$85.00/$110.00/$135.00

No. 4670 Mack Trailers
1929 – 1932, rare
$125.00/$150.00/$200.00 each

Unnumbered 1928 Model A Mail
1931 – 1933, sold in sets only
$85.00/$100.00/$115.00

No. 0133 1934 Ford Wrecker
3", 1934 – 1935
$80.00/$100.00/$120.00

No. 0133 1935 Ford Wrecker
3", 1935 – 1941
$65.00/$75.00/$85.00

No. 0120 Oil Tanker
3", 1936 – 1939
$60.00/$70.00/$80.00

No. 0121 1936 Ford Pickup
3", 1936 – 1939
$60.00/$70.00/$80.00

No. 0123 1936 Special Delivery
3", 1937 – 1939
$70.00 $80.00/$90.00

No. 1006 Standard Oil
6", 1939 – 1941
$60.00/$75.00/$90.00

No. 1006 Standard Oil
6", 1947
$55.00/$65.00/$75.00

No. 1007 Sinclair Oil
6", 1939 – 1941
$60.00/$75.00/$90.00

No. 1007 Sinclair Oil,
6", 1947
$55.00/$65.00/$75.00

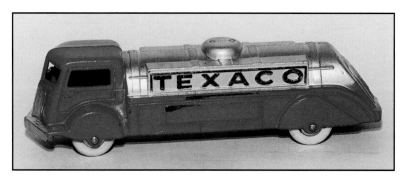

No. 1008 Texaco Oil
6", 1939 – 1941
$65.00/$75.00/$85.00

No. 1008 Texaco Oil
6", 1947
$60.00/$70.00/$80.00

No. 1009 Shell Oil
6", 1939 – 1941
$65.00/$75.00/$85.00

No. 1009 Shell Oil
6", 1947
$60.00/$70.00/$80.00

No. 1010 Wrigley's Box Van
4", 1940 – 1941
$75.00/$110.00/$125.00

No. 1010 Box Van
4", 1948
$55.00/$75.00/$95.00

No. 1019 Jumbo Pickup
6", 1936 – 1941
$45.00/$55.00/$65.00

No. 1019 Jumbo Pickup
6", 1942 – 1946
$35.00/$45.00/$55.00

No. 1027 Jumbo Wrecker
6", 1937 – 1941
$55.00/$65.00/$75.00

No. 1027 Jumbo Wrecker
6", 1942 – 1946
$45.00/$55.00/$65.00

No. 1040 Hook & Ladder
4", 1937 – 1941
$70.00/$80.00/$90.00

No. 1041 Hose Car
4", 1937 – 1938, no man rear
$65.00/$75.00/$85.00

No. 1041 Hose Car
4", 1939 – 1941
$60.00/$70.00/$80.00

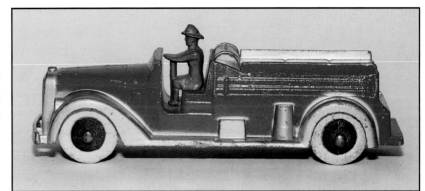

No. 1042 Insurance Patrol
4", 1937 – 1938
$65.00/$75.00/$85.00

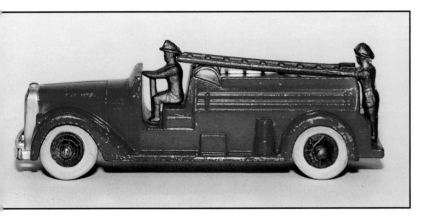

No. 1042 Insurance Patrol
4", 1939 – 1941
$60.00/$70.00/$80.00

No. 234 Box Truck
3", 1940 – 1941
$20.00/$25.00/$30.00

No. 234 Box Truck
3", 1947 – 1948
$15.00/$20.00/$25.00

No. 235 Oil Tanker
3", 1940 – 1941, two caps top
$20.00/$25.00/$30.00

No. 235 Oil Tanker
3", 1947 – 1948, two caps top
$20.00/$25.00/$30.00

No. 235 Oil Tanker
3", 1947 – 1954, four caps top
$20.00/$25.00/$30.00

No. 236 Hook & Ladder
3", 1940 – 1941, rare with ladder
$45.00/$55.00/$65.00

No. 236 Hook & Ladder
3", 1947 – 1948, postwar
$40.00/$50.00/$60.00

No. 237 Insurance Patrol
3", 1940 – 1941
$40.00/$50.00/$60.00

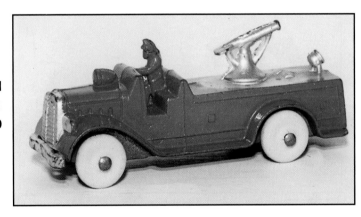

No. 237 Insurance Patrol
3", 1947 – 1948
$35.00/$45.00/$55.00

No. 238 Hose Wagon
3", 1940 – 1941
$40.00/$50.00/$60.00

No. 238 Hose Wagon
3", 1947 – 1948
$35.00/$45.00/$55.00

1949 American La France Pumper
3", 1949 – 1959
$20.00/$25.00/$30.00

1949 American La France Pumper
3", 1949 – 1959
Note: Axles inside fenders
$20.00/$25.00/$30.00

1956 Chevy Cameo Pickup
4", 1959 – 1969
$25.00/$30.00/$35.00

1950 Chevy Panel
4", 1950 – 1953
Open rear windows
$30.00/$40.00/$50.00

1950 Chevy Panel
4",1950 – 1953
Closed rear windows
$35.00/$45.00/$55.00

1950 Chevy Panel
4", 1950 – 1953, rare two-tone
$35.00/$45.00/$55.00

1950 Chevy Ambulance
4", 1953 – 1960
Open rear windows
$35.00/$45.00/$55.00

1950 Chevy Ambulance
4", 1953 – 1960, closed rear window
$40.00/$50.00/$60.00

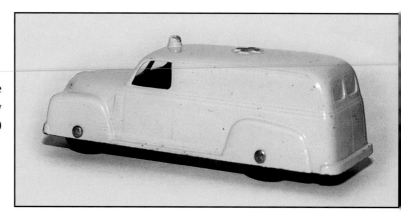

1950 Chevy Panel
3", 1950 – 1959, open and closed rear window
$20.00/$25.00/$30.00

1950 Chevy Panel
3", 1950 – 1959, open and closed rear window
Note: Open front fenders
$20.00/$25.00/$30.00

1960 Chevy El Camino
6", 1960 – 1967
$30.00/$40.00/$50.00

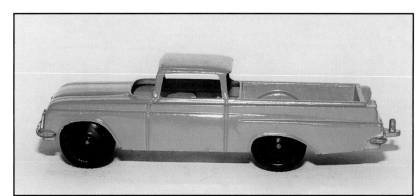

1960 Chevy El Camino
6", 1962 – 1964, camper and boat rare
$80.00/$90.00/$100.00

1956 Dodge Panel
6", 1959 – 1966
$55.00/$65.00/$75.00

1956 Dodge Panel
6", 1959 – 1966, with tin bottom
$70.00/$85.00/$100.00

1950 Dodge Pickup
4", open small windows
$25.00/$30.00/$35.00

1947 Hudson Pickup
4", 1947 – 1949, rare
$50.00/$60.00/$70.00

1950 Dodge Pickup
4", 1950 – 1960, closed small windows
$25.00/$30.00/$35.00

1955 Ford C600 Oil
3", 1955 – 1960
$20.00/$25.00/$30.00

1962 Ford C600 Oil
5½", 1962 – 1966
$25.00/$30.00/$35.00

Ford Econoline
5½", 1962
$25.00/$30.00/$35.00

1949 Ford F1 Pickup
3", 1949 – 1960, closed tailgate
$25.00/$30.00/$35.00

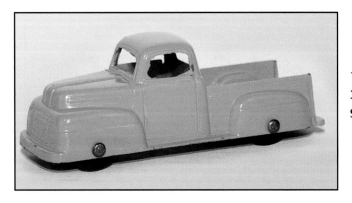

1949 Ford F1 Pickup
3", 1949 – 1960, open tailgate
$20.00/$25.00/$30.00

1949 Ford F1 Pickup
3", 1949 – 1960, closed rear window, rare
$30.00/$40.00/$50.00

1949 Ford F1 Pickup
3", 1949 – 1960, type 2
$15.00/$20.00/$25.00

1949 Ford Texaco Oil Tanker
6", 1949 – 1952
$45.00/$55.00/$65.00

1949 Shell Ford Oil Tanker
6", 1949 – 1952, also in yellow
$45.00/$55.00/$65.00

1949 Ford F6
4", 1950 – 1969, also with silver bed
$20.00/$25.00/$30.00

1949 Ford F6
4", 1960 – 1969, open fenders
$15.00/$20.00/$25.00

1949 Ford F6 Oil
4", 1950 – 1969, sleeve axles
$20.00/$25.00/$30.00

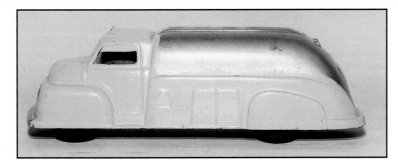

1949 Ford F6 Oil
4", 1960 – 1969, axles inside fenders
$15.00/$20.00/$25.00

1957 Ford Styleside Pickup
3", 1959 – 1964, 1968 – 1969
Open and closed rear window
$20.00/$25.00/$30.00

1956 Ford F700 Stake Truck
6", 1960 – 1964
$30.00/$35.00/$40.00

1956 Ford 700 Stake
6", 1960 – 1964, with tin cap top
$60.00/$80.00/$100.00

International K1 Panel
4", 1947 – 1949
$35.00/$45.00/$55.00

International K1 Ambulance
4", 1947 – 1949, rare
$50.00/$60.00/$70.00

International K11 Sincair Oil
6", 1949 – 1955
$45.00/$55.00/$65.00

International K11 Standard Oil
6", 1949 – 1955
$50.00/$60.00/$70.00

International Metro Van
6", 1959 only, very rare
$125.00/$150.00/$175.00

1947 International K5 Stake
6", 1947 – 1953, open sides
$35.00/$40.00/$45.00

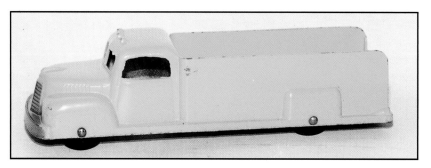

1947 International K5 Stake
6", 1953, closed sides
Note: With and without ribbed bed
$45.00/$55.00/$65.00

International Car Transport
1947 – 1954
Note: Yellow trailers also
$55.00/$65.00/$75.00

International Car Transport
1955 – 1958
Note: Oval openings on trailer
$45.00/$55.00/$65.00

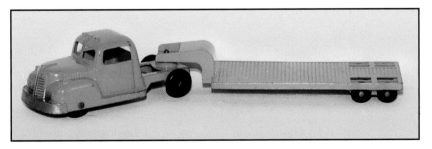

1947 International K5 Gooseneck Trailer
1949 – 1958
$40.00/$45.00/$55.00

1947 International K5 Grain Hauler
1949 – 1958
$35.00/$45.00/$55.00

1947 International K5 TOOTSIETOY Semi
1949 – 1958
$50.00/$55.00/$60.00

1948 International Bottle Truck
6", 1949 – 1958, rare
$60.00/$70.00/$80.00

1947 International K5 Dump Truck
6", 1948 – 1953
$40.00/$45.00/$50.00

1947 International K5 Tow Truck
6", 1948 – 1952
$40.00/$45.00/$50.00

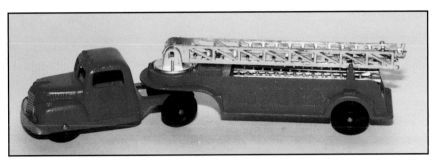

International K5 Hook & Ladder
8½", 1953 – 1955, rare
No. 5211 Fire boxed set only
$80.00/$90.00/$100.00

1947 Mack L-Line Dump Truck
6", 1954 – 1966
Note: Rubber and plastic tires, rare
$35.00/$40.00/$45.00

1947 Mack L-Line Tow Truck
5½", 1954 – 1966
$25.00/$35.00/$45.00

1947 Mack L-Line Fire Pumper
6", 1953 – 1958, rare
$55.00/$65.00/$75.00 rare

Mack L-Line Van Trailer
1954 – 1959
Note: Many custom logos
$100.00/$125.00/$150.00

(More examples in Private Advertising Semis chapter)

Mack L-Line Van TOOTSIETOY Trailer
1954 – 1959
$75.00/$100.00/$125.00

Mack L-Line Oil Tanker
1954 – 1959
Note: Ladder rear of trailer
$75.00/$85.00/$95.00

Mack L-Line Log Truck
1955 – 1959, 1961, 1963 – 1965
$75.00/$85.00/$95.00

1947 Mack L-Line Machine Hauler
1956 – 1960
$75.00/$100.00/$125.00

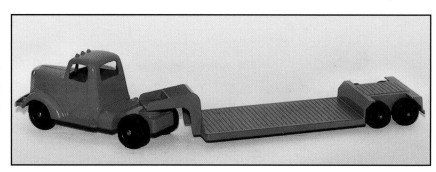

1947 Mack L-Line Stakeside Trailer
1954 – 1959
$100.00/$125.00/$150.00

Mack L-Line TOOTSIETOY Oil Tanker
1954 – 1959
Note: Has red cab and silver trailer also
$90.00/$110.00/$130.00

Mack L-Line TOOTSIETOY Van Trailer
1954 – 1959, open casting rear, no doors
$90.00/$110.00/$130.00

Mack L-Line Hook and Ladder
1956 – 1961, 1963 – 1967
Rubber and plastic tires
$110.00/$125.00/$135.00

Mack L-Line with its TOOTSIETOY tin cap on
1958 – 1959
$70.00/$95.00/$120.00

Mack L-Line Stepside Stake,
6", 1954 – 1957
$45.00/$55.00/$65.00

Mack L-Line Stake
6", 1958 – 1959, even sided
$45.00/$55.00/$65.00

Mack L-Line Semi and Utility Trailer
9", 1960 – 1963
$90.00/$100.00/$110.00

1947 Mack L-Line Pipe Truck
9", years unknown, rare
Note: Silver plastic pipes
$100.00/$120.00/$140.00

1955 Mack B-Line Cement Truck
6"
Note: First type worm axle to rotate barrel
$45.00/$55.00/$65.00

1955 Mack B-Line Cement Truck
6", 1959 – 1969
Note: Second type, no trim, straight axles, and
no worm
$40.00/$50.00/$60.00

1955 Mack B-Line Utility Trailer
9", 1960 – 1963
$70.00/$90.00/$110.00

1955 Mack B-Line Log Truck
9", 1960, 1967
$70.00/$80.00/$90.00

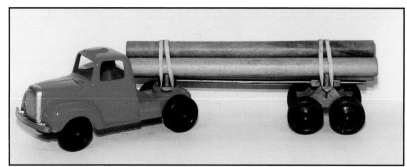

1955 Mack B-Line MOBIL Oil Tanker
1960 – 1965, 1967 – 1969
$65.00/$75.00/$85.00

1955 Mack B-Line MOBILGAS Oil Tanker,
years unknown, rare
$100.00/$120.00/$140.00

Mack B-Line TOOTSIETOY Oil Tanker
9", 1960 – 1967
$80.00/$100.00/$120.00

RC 180 Machine Hauler
1963 – 1966, semi-rare truck
$65.00/$75.00/$85.00

RC 180 Oil Tanker
9", 1962,
$55.00/$65.00/$75.00

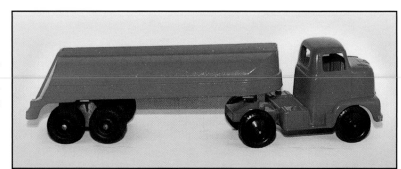

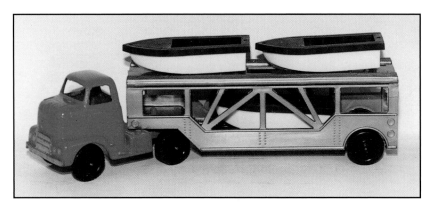

RC 180 Boat Transport
With three boats and ramp
1962 – 1967
$100.00/$125.00/$150.00

RC 180 Auto Transport
1962 – 1964, 1968
plastic trailer-like boat transport
$60.00/$70.00/$80.00

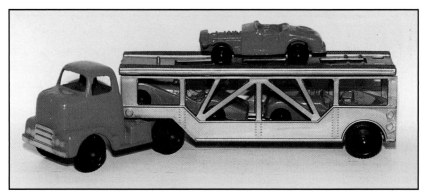

RC 180 Dean Van Lines
1963 – 1964, 1967, plastic trailer
$100.00/$125.00/$150.00

RC 180 Auto Transport
1959 – 1961, Tin ramp, dual axle trailer
$100.00/$125.00/$150.00

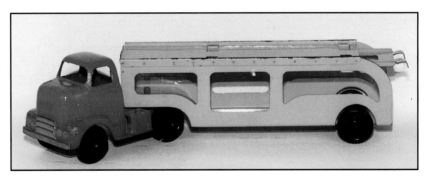

RC 180 Transport
1959 – 1961, tin ramp, single axle trailer
$90.00/$110.00/$150.00

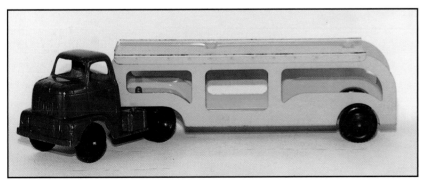

RC 180 Auto Transport
1959 – 1961, last version no ramp
and silver trim cab
$75.00/$190.00/$105.00

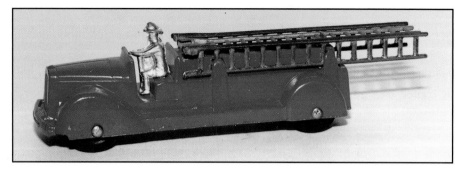

No. 1040 Hook and Ladder
4", 1942, 1946, 1948, postwar, rare
$85.00/$100.00/$115.00

No. 1041 Hose Car
4", 1948 only, postwar
$100.00/$125.00/$150.00

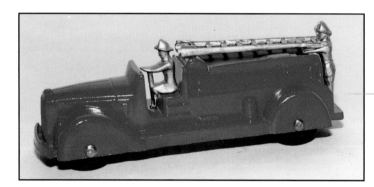

No. 1042 Insurance Patrol
4", 1948 only, postwar, rarest of three types
$100.00/$125.00/$150.00

No. 108 Caterpillar
No. 105 Oil Tanker
No. 109 Stake Truck
No. 104 Insurance Patrol
2", 1932 – 1934
$35.00/$45.00/$55.00

1959 Chevrolet Tractor Semis

The cab over engine 1959 Chevrolet cab made its debut in the 1965 Tootsietoy catalog. Several types of these rare trucks last appeared in Strombecker Corporation's 1966 toy catalog.

The new visually packed Toosietoy sets of assorted vehicles with accessories sold for $1.00. The only truck that came with extra pieces was the No. 2969 TOOTSIETOY ARMY SET. It came with a truck cab, lowboy trailer, 3" CJ3 Jeep, and three soft plastic infantry soldiers. Truck and trailer were painted Army green along with the CJ3 Jeep that sat on the trailer's bed.

The No. 2944 TOOTSIETOY MOVING VAN was decaled Dean Van Lines, the cab, painted white with blue grill and bumper trim, the trailer a white rugged plastic with opening door at the rear. This 1959 van was nine inches long roughly like all the other following trucks in this chapter.

The No. 2917 TOOTSIE TOY BOAT TRANSPORT set consisted of a cab pulling a plastic open trailer hauling three colorful boats also made of plastic. The trailers and boats I've seen in several color combinations to date.

the No. 2920 TOOTSIETOY AUTO TRANSPORT set consisted of five pieces: the metal cab, open plastic trailer, plastic ramp, and two 3" metal cars. My catalog shows the TR3 roadster with a 1960 Ford Falcon on top of the trailer's deck.

The No. 4360 TOOTSIETOY AMERICAN ROAD SET, new in the 1965 catalog, contained auto, boat transports with their loads, and the large Scenicruiser bus still mint in the box. Can you ever imagine finding this rare set with two 1959 Chevrolet transports and bus still mint in the box?

The 1966 catalog no longer showed the No. 4360 AMERICAN ROAD SET and the No. 2969 ARMY SET. Three totally new 1959 Chevrolet trucks with trailers were added to the line in its catalog. They were the Mobil oil, log, and Hook and Ladder fire truck. The Dean Van Lines, boat, and auto transports continued in 1966 company catalogs.

The No. 2820 TOOTSIETOY MOBIL OIL TANKER was painted a reddish orange, both cab and trailer to match. Three Mobil sticker graced the trailer's body.

The No. 2830 TOOTSIETOY LOGGER truck came with five removable wooden logs held onto a frame trailer by two rubber bands.

The No. 2905 TOOTSIETOY HOOK & LADDER FIRE TRUCK came with a matching painted trailer supporting an adjustable extension ladder assembly of two ladders.

This concludes all the many types of 1959 Chevrolet cab semis. You may use any of the trailers from Mack B, Mack L, and RC 180 trailers with a loose cab and put together you or own set, in the event your lucky enough to find a loose cab in any condition.

No. 2944
Tootsietoy Moving Van
1965 – 1966
No price available

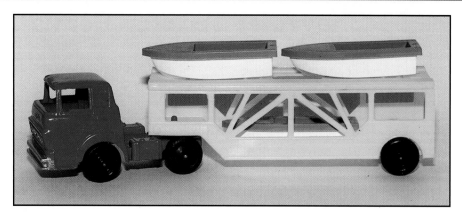

No. 2917
Tootsietoy Boat Transport
1965 – 1966
No price available

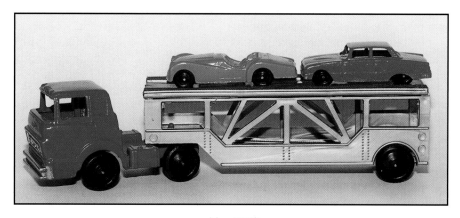

No. 2920
Tootsietoy Auto Transport
1965 – 1966
No price available

No. 2820
Tootsietoy Mobil Oil Tanker
1966
No price available

No. 2830
Tootsietoy Logger Truck
1966
No price available

No. 2905
Tootsietoy Hook & Ladder Fire Truck
1966
No price available

Private Advertising Semis

Private decaled or stickered trucks are an interesting group of toys to collect. They are my favorite post-war trucks. The only trucks advertised in Strombecker Corporation catalogs were their Tootsietoy Line and the Dean Van Lines.

Lets talk about the 1947 Mack trucks with private logos. The cabs on the trucks had private logos. The cabs on the trucks were painted red, green, or black and were dressed with silver trim fronts. Two types of tires were used with the sleeve and nail axles both on the cab and trailers. The first type were rubber tires and the later were plastic tires with Tootsietoy logos on the outer rims. The trailer had a single casting for the floor and sides. Two small rear doors were put into small holes on the floor and upper cross braces held the top of the doors. A top made of tin covered the trailer and locking the doors in place. The trailer had its wheel supports flared to the bed or rear floor of trailer. After the truck was completed the private decals or stickers were attached to both sides of the trailer. They were then put into a Tootsietoy box for the retailer or private companies to distribute. The 1947 Mack B-Line cabs pulled many of Strombecker's truck trailers and also private labeled ones. The only examples that I am aware of are Borden's Milk and Union Carbide Chemicals. Both cabs came with and without silver trim on the grill fronts. The later cab had a horn cast on the roof of the truck cab. The trailers were hollow underneath, with the four axle post supports cast with the trailer's body.

The RC 1801 Westinghouse is the only example I have to show you. I'm sure others may exist with different private logos. The trailer is plastic like the Dean Van Lines, with a single hinged plastic door at rear of the trailer.

All of the following trucks were purchased for between $100.00 and $200.00 plus, either at toy shows or from private collectors. Please feel free to write me about or send me a photo of any private labeled semi not shown. Keep on trucking!

Tootsitetoy Line

Libby's

Gerard Motors Express

Middle States Motor Freight Inc.

M. A. Soper Co.

Olson Transportation Co.

Huber and Huber Motor Express Co.

Spector

Borden's Milk Tanker

Union Carbide Chemicals Tanker

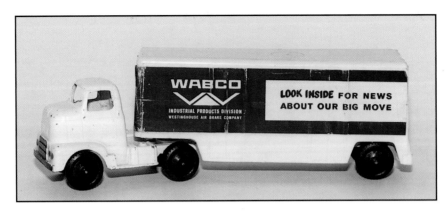

Westinghouse

Dean Van Lines

Mobilgas Tanker

Nutmeg Oil Tanker

HO Bargin Town U. S. A.

HO Meijer Foods

HO Turn ✴ Style

HO Coast to Coast Stores

Stratton Express Service

Seventies Tootsietoys
1970 – 1979

During the 1970s Strombecker Corporation carried several of its later 1960s toys with the new toys of the 1970s. Different color schemes, packaging, and some decals were the most obvious changes to their vehicle line up. Every year Strombecker added many new single toys that were sold separately and placed into the various boxed sets.

The Strombecker Corporation had many Tootsietoy midgets that were sold in bulk for the dealers. They were assorted models of unbreakable die-cast metal cars and trucks with steel axles and roll-easy wheels. The toys were roughly 2½" in length and painted in all the popular colors — red, yellow, light blue, dark blue, silver, green, orange, and the light and dark purples. The tiny midgets were placed in many different series and boxed sets. The Collector Series sets usually had a car or truck pulling a small metal trailer with a plastic yacht. A small metal trailer containing a small plastic motorcycle and others were used to make this series somewhat special. The tiny Midgets were also packaged in Jam Pacs™ and placed into activity sets; No. 1750 Activity Garage, No. 1780 Exclusive Tootsietoy Service Station with its own carrying case. We can't forget the popular No. 1249 Little Toughs truck and trailer assortments. Many models have trailer hooks to pull the different trailers. These were easily broken off by being mishandled. I will try to show you all of the Midgets and their packaging in this chapter. These are the most common toys to be found at garage sales and flea markets. Toys still in their original packaging or boxed sets are really rare to stumble onto, but like all other toys the fun is in the search.

Two new assortments were added to the terrific Strombecker line in 1970. They were the No. 1290 Assortment consisting of six trucks and Jeepsters in two body styles. The No. 1295 Assortment also had six different vehicles. This assortment contained a VW, school bus, resort bus, Ford Bronco, dune buggy with surf boards, and an Attex all terrain vehicle. Tootsietoy TOUGHS™ were die-cast cars and trucks with realistic detail: bumpers, seats, and chassis. The overall length was 4" for these toys. Tires for these toys were polypropylene wheels with white plastic centered hubs.

These pieces with different paint schemes and decals or stickers were placed in many of the gift sets and packaged separately: No. 1747 Fire Fighters and No. 1840 "Road Master" to mention just two. The No. 1745 Hitch-Up™ sets were made up of many vehicles pulling trailers with all sorts of boats, motorcycles, and sport vehicles. The first Hitch-Up Series™ had eight different 4" vehicles pulling different Tootsietoy accessories. The No. 2535 Tootsietoy Farm Tractor and Spreader was added to this popular line in 1970 as a new item.

The tractor with spreader is the hardest piece to come by and the Ford Bronco by far is the easiest to obtain for your collection.

Tootsietoy Road Haulers consisted of eight different trucks ranging in length from 6½" to 8¼" depending on the trailer length. The same tractor or semi cab was used for the Log Truck, Auto Transport, and the Horse Trailer. The No. 2545 Hook and Ladder is the most common piece in this series of vehicles. Beware, the fire truck will not always have all its white plastic ladders.

The hardest vehicle to find in the Road Hauler Series is No. 1930 Tootsietoy, "Double Bottom Dumper." The set had a small HO scale cab pulling dumper trailers. This is a prime example of a toy carried into the 1970s by Strombecker Corporation. It appeared only in the 1971 and 1972 toy catalogs.

Tootsietoy® Playmates, "Big Slicks," Hop'd Rods, Super Slicks™, Freakies, and many more sets and series were offered in Strombecker catalogs. Road racing sets, cap guns, rifles, pistols, and many of the all plastic vehicles were offered between 1970 and 1979.

Examples of almost all Tootsietoy vehicles and some packaged toys and sets will now grace the following pages. In my opinion, the Collector Series with its HO scaled trucks with trailers, the different hydraulic cranes, as well as the colorful Playmate sets, will be good sets of toys to collect.

For this chapter of my book, I have collected as many examples as possible. However, for the pieces I have not been able to purchase for my collection, I used a few Strombecker color catalog pages.

Happy collecting!

1010 and 1011 Tootsietoy Midgets

Pumper, Jeep Truck, 40 Ford, Panel Truck
1970 – 1977
$2.00/$3.00/$4.00

El Camino, MG, Hot Rod, T-Bird
1970 – 1977
$2.00/$3.00/$4.00

Shuttle Truck, Ford J Tow Truck, Oil Truck
1970 – 1977
$2.00/$3.00/$4.00

Volkswagon, Jeep, D-Jaguar, Mustang
1970 – 1977
$2.00/$3.00/$4.00

Porche, Earth Mover, Cadillac, Cheetah
1970 – 1977
$2.00/$3.00/$4.00

Jeepster Pick-up, Mercedes, Corvette, Formula I
1970 – 1977
$2.00/$3.00/$4.00

1055 Die-cast Airplanes

West German McDonnell F4C "PHANTOM II"
1970 – 1977
$6.00/$8.00/$10.00

French Dassault IIC "MIRAGE"
1970 – 1977
$6.00/$8.00/$10.00

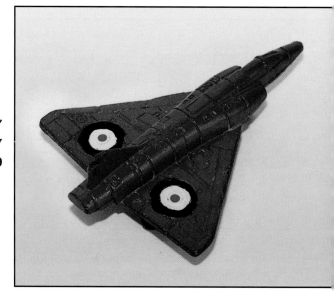

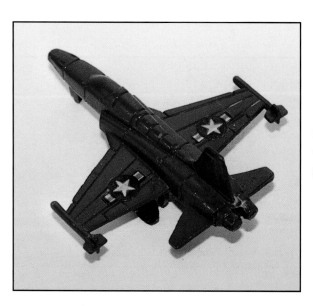

U.S. Northrop F5A "LITTLE TIGER"
1970 – 1975
$6.00/$8.00/$10.00

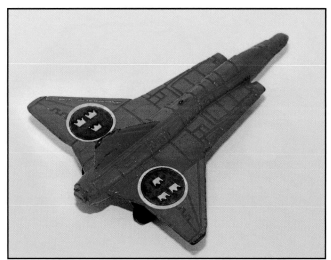

Swedish Saab J35 "DRAGON"
1970 – 1975
$6.00/$8.00/$10.00

1290 Trucks and Jeeps

Shell Oil Truck
1970 – 1979
$8.00/$10.00/$12.00

"JUMPIN JEEPER" Jeespter
1970 – 1979
$8.00/$10.00/$12.00

Pumper Fire Truck
1970 – 1979
$8.00/$10.00/$12.00

"WILD WAGON"
1970 – 1979
$8.00/$10.00/$12.00

"WHEELIE WAGON"
1970 – 1979
$8.00/$10.00/$12.00

Jeep
1970 – 1979
$8.00/$10.00/$12.00

1295 Car Assortment

"STINGING BUG" VW
1970 – 1979
$8.00/$10.00/$12.00

"BUZY BEE" School Bus
1970 – 1979
$8.00/$10.00/$12.00

"BIMINI BUGGY" Resort Bug
1970 – 1979
$8.00/$10.00/$12.00

"BUCKIN BRONCO" Ford
1970 – 1979
$8.00/$10.00/$12.00

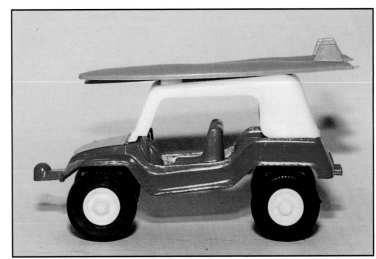

Dune Buggy
1970 – 1979
$8.00/$10.00/$12.00

ATTEX All Terrain Vehicle
1970 – 1979
$8.00/$10.00/$12.00

1438 (1970) 1249 Little Toughs
(1971 – 1979)

Semi-truck with Cab
1970 – 1979
$10.00/$15.00/$20.00

Logger with Cab
1970 – 1979
$10.00/$15.00/$20.00

Mobil Gas Tanker
1970
$10.00/$15.00/$20.00

American La France Fire Engine
1970 – 1979
$10.00/$15.00/$20.00

Aerial Ladder Fire Truck
1970
$10.00/$15.00/$20.00

Dump Truck
1970
$10.00/$15.00/$20.00

Cement Truck
1970
$10.00/$15.00/$20.00

Jeep with Racer, Trailer
1970 – 1979
$8.00/$10.00/$12.00

El Camino with Boat, Trailer
1970 – 1979
$8.00/$10.00/$12.00

Collector Series

1451 Farm Tracker with Utility Wagon
1970
$20.00/$25.00/$30.00

1452 Heavy Duty Hydraulic Crane
1970
$20.00/$25.00/$30.00

1456 Honda Motorcycle with trailer and truck
1970
$8.00/$10.00/$12.00

1460 Auto Transport
1970 – 1979
$20.00/$25.00/$30.00

1468 Car and Cabin Cruizer
1970 – 1997
$10.00/$15.00/$20.00

1469 Truck and Horse Trailer
1970
$30.00/$35.00/$40.00

Hitch-up Series™ Vehicles

2522 K-9 Hitch-up
1970 – 1971
Note: Eight dogs and clear dome missing
$15.00/$20.00/$25.00

(Complete packaged toy shown on page 25

2523 Honda Hitch-up
1970 – 1975
$10.00/$15.00/$20.00

2524 Cabin Cruizer Hitch-up
1970 – 1976
$10.00/$15.00/$20.00

2525 U-Haul Hitch-up
1970 – 1976
$10.00/$15.00/$20.00

2527 Beach Buggy Hitch-up
1970 – 1975
$10.00/$15.00/$20.00

2528 Snowmobile Hitch-up
1970 – 1975
$25.00/$30.00/$35.00

2529 ATTEX® Hitch-up
1970 – 1976
$10.00/$15.00/$20.00

2535 Farm Tractor and Spreader
1970 – 1973
$20.00/$25.00/$30.00

jam pac™

2831 BLISTER CARDED "JAM PAC"™. New blister carded Jam Pac cars and trucks on a bright illustrated card. 8 die-cast cars packed under a clear, case style, blister. Size 4¹/₂" x 12¹/₂" packed in shelf display box, (see page 12) 3 dozen to display carton, weight 18 lbs.

2834 TOOTSIETOY "JAM PAC™ FLEET". "Jam Pac Fleet" is displayed in a 3³/₄" x 14" frame view box with a formed plastic tray to show the product to its best advantage. Each fleet includes 8 die-cast metal cars and trucks and a set of 3 gas pumps on an island. Pumps have flexible hoses and storage hooks for nozzles. 1 dz. to master carton, weight 6 lbs.

2835 TOOTSIETOY "JAM-PAC"™. 10 top selling die-cast metal miniature cars and trucks. Each is realistically scaled to produce fine detail. Brightly colored assortment is packed in a new, all visual, frame view, package. 1 dz. "JAM-PAC"™ to master carton, weight 6 lbs.

2835

2831

2834

die cast planes & trains

2850 JET FIGHTERS. 3 die-cast replicas of popular fighter jets with colorful authentic wing markings. Models include Swedish Saab J 35 "Dragon," U. S. Northrop F 5A "Little Tiger," West German McDonnell F4C "Phantom" and French Dassault IIIC "Mirage." 1 dz. to carton, weight 5 lbs.

2855 TRAIN. 6-piece, highly detailed, train measures 16" overall. Hitches together easily for pull-along play. Cars include diesel engine, coal car, reefer, covered hopper, cattle car and caboose. 1 dz. to carton, weight 6¹/₂ lbs.

2850 JET FIGHTERS.

2855 TRAIN.

1971 catalog page showing JAM PAC™, die-cast planes and trains
2831 Blister carded – $35.00
2834 Tootsie Fleet – $35.00
2835 Tootsie carded – $40.00
2850 Jet Fighters – $35.00
2855 Train (6 piece) – $50.00

Tootsietoy® Road Haulers

2940 Dump Truck
6¼", 1970 – 1979
$10.00/$15.00/$20.00

2941 Sanitation Truck
6¼", 1970 – 1979
$10.00/$15.00/$20.00

2543 Cement Truck
6", 1970 – 1979
$10.00/$15.00/$20.00

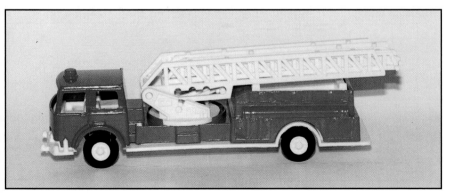

2545 Hook & Ladder
7¼", 1970 – 1974
$10.00/$15.00/$20.00

2550 Logger
7½", 1970 – 1975
$10.00/$15.00/$20.00

2555 Horse Trailer
8¼", 1970 – 1975
$15.00/$20.00/$25.00

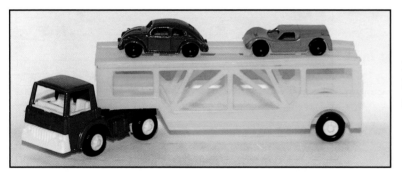

2920 Auto Transport
8½", 1970 – 1975
$15.00/$20.00/$25.00

1930 "Double Bottom Dumper"
1970, 1971, rare
$25.00/$30.00/$35.00

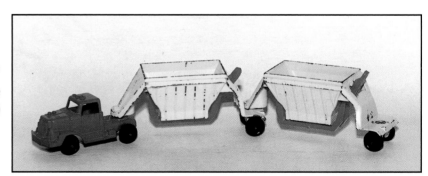

Tootsietoy Playmates

2024 Tommy Tractor
6½", 1970 – 1972
$20.00/$25.00/$30.00

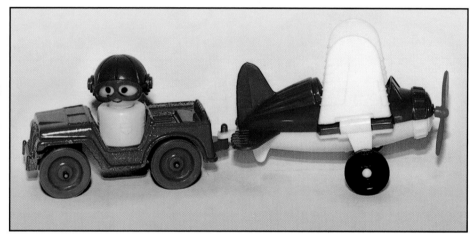

2025 Peter Pilot
7", 1970 – 1972
$20.00/$25.00/$30.00

2026 Ronnie Racer
6½", 1970 – 1972
$20.00/$25.00/$30.00

TOOTSIETOY®
super slicks™

2944 SUPER SLICKS™. Six assorted "wayout" custom style fun cars. Features include "Sculptured Look" die-cast metal bodies, beautiful show color paint, super wide slick racing tires, chrome plated wheels and engines, interior detail, steering wheel, decals and windshields. Assortment includes Pie Wagon, Twin Shaft, Dune Buster, Desert Fox, Bandito, and Panzer Wagon. Size of cars 4¼". All Blister packed on crazy color cards. 1 dozen to carton. Weight 4 lbs.

DUNE BUSTER

DESERT FOX

PANZER WAGON

TWIN SHAFT

BANDITO

PIE WAGON

Catalog page showing SUPER SLICKS™
1971 – 1976
$10.00/$15.00/$20.00

2950 Freakies

"SWEAT-T"
1970 – 1973
$15.00/$20.00/$25.00

"DRAGON DRAGSTER"
1970 – 1973
$15.00/$20.00/$25.00

"TIJUANA TARANTULA"
1970 – 1973
$15.00/$20.00/$25.00

2019 Delivery Trucks

Mickey Milk
1971
$45.00 MIP

Farmer Jones
1971
$45.00 MIP

Hoky Smoky
1971
$45.00 MIP

activity sets

1750 ACTIVITY GARAGE. A modern automatic Super Service Station with action features. Car wash section has turntable, push rod, and crank. Tihs assembly moves the car through 3 sponge wash rollers. When car has been washed it will roll down ramp through "CRASH CORNER" intersection. Station has a fast car start lane with spring loaded push button release. Elevating grease ramp for car lubrication. Service station building has side windows and skylights. 6 gasoline pumps with moveable hoses. 4 die-cast metal cars and trucks complete the fun. Size 2¹/₂x8x11. 6 each to carton, weight 4 lbs.

1751 SUPER AIRPORT. The world's busiest airport all in one package. ACTION, ACTION, ACTION. Airport control panel activates the set. Right hand throttle handle raises inspection ramp inside of hanger for engine inspection; reverse handle and plane will roll down ramp. Push left hand throttle and airplane will turn 180° on vector selector turntable until operator selects runway direction desired. Turn the roll out control and aircraft will slowly move out onto the field. Load plane catapult and push release button for fast take-off. Brightly colored and checker-board decorated. Hanger comes complete with 3 die-cast metal airplanes. Size 3¹/₂x8x11. 6 each to carton, weight 4 lbs.

1780 EXCLUSIVE TOOTSIETOY SERVICE STATION CARRYING CASE. Unique service station folds up into easily transported carrying case. Station is made of high-impact plastic with pull-out car ramp. Cars may travel up the ramp to second floor parking area. Garage doors lift up and down. Case opens to form a generous service area complete with 10 Tootsietoy cars, illustrated gas pumps, oil racks, and roadways. Carrying handle on side of case. Size 2¹/₂"x5"x12". Packed 12 each to master carton, weight 26 lbs.

CASE SHOWN OPEN

COMPLETE WITH 10 CARS

CASE FOLDS INTO COMPACT CARRYING CASE

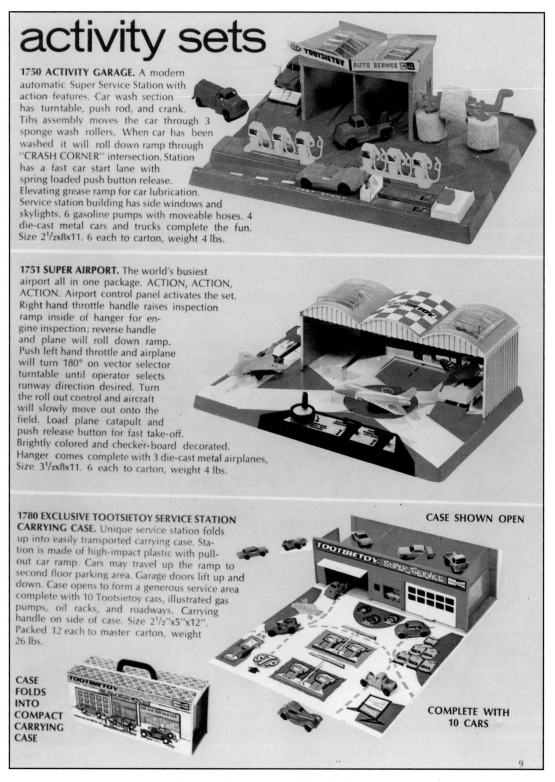

9

1971 catalog page, ACTIVITY SETS
1970 – 1971
1750 Activity Garage – $75.00
1751 Super Airport – $75.00
1780 Service Station – $75.00

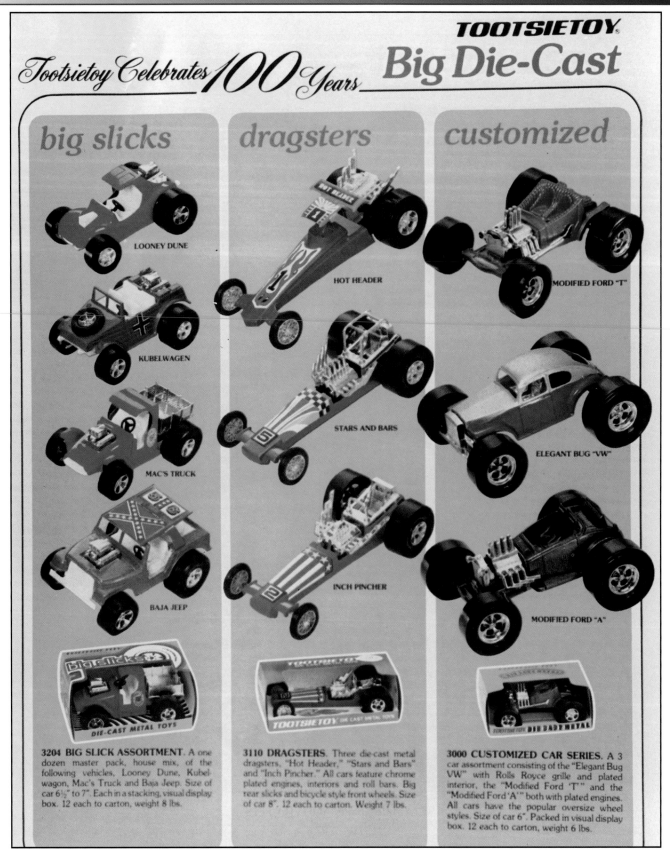

Tootsietoy Celebrates 100 Years

TOOTSIETOY.
Big Die-Cast

big slicks

LOONEY DUNE

KUBELWAGEN

MAC'S TRUCK

BAJA JEEP

dragsters

HOT HEADER

STARS AND BARS

INCH PINCHER

customized

MODIFIED FORD "T"

ELEGANT BUG "VW"

MODIFIED FORD "A"

3204 BIG SLICK ASSORTMENT. A one dozen master pack, house mix, of the following vehicles, Looney Dune, Kubelwagon, Mac's Truck and Baja Jeep. Size of car 6½" to 7". Each in a stacking, visual display box. 12 each to carton, weight 8 lbs.

3110 DRAGSTERS. Three die-cast metal dragsters, "Hot Header," "Stars and Bars" and "Inch Pincher." All cars feature chrome plated engines, interiors and roll bars. Big rear slicks and bicycle style front wheels. Size of car 8". 12 each to carton. Weight 7 lbs.

3000 CUSTOMIZED CAR SERIES. A 3 car assortment consisting of the "Elegant Bug VW" with Rolls Royce grille and plated interior, the "Modified Ford 'T'" and the "Modified Ford 'A'" both with plated engines. All cars have the popular oversize wheel styles. Size of car 6". Packed in visual display box. 12 each to carton, weight 6 lbs.

3400 BIG SLICKS, 3100 DRAGSTERS 1972 – 1976, CUSTOMIZED 1974 – 1976
3204 – $10.00/$15.00/$20.00 3110 – $10.00/$15.00/$20.00 300.00 – $10.00/$15.00/$20.00

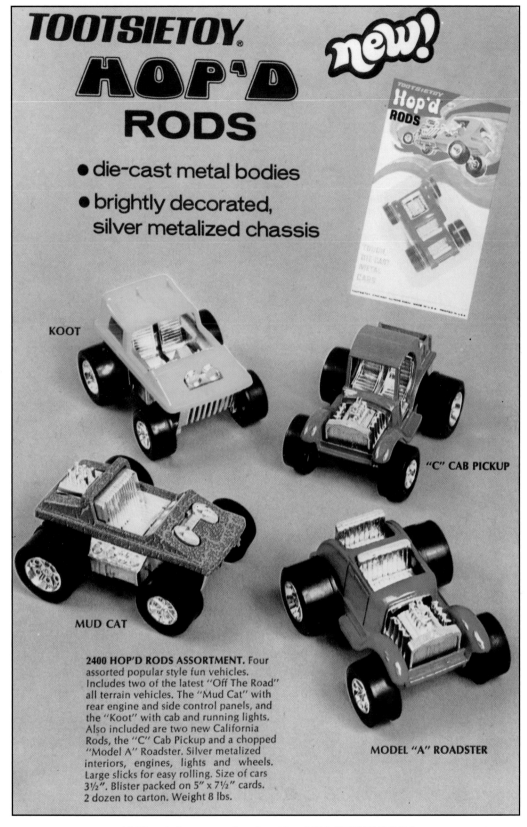

TOOTSIETOY HOP'D RODS

new!

- die-cast metal bodies
- brightly decorated, silver metalized chassis

KOOT

"C" CAB PICKUP

MUD CAT

2400 HOP'D RODS ASSORTMENT. Four assorted popular style fun vehicles. Includes two of the latest "Off The Road" all terrain vehicles. The "Mud Cat" with rear engine and side control panels, and the "Koot" with cab and running lights. Also included are two new California Rods, the "C" Cab Pickup and a chopped "Model A" Roadster. Silver metalized interiors, engines, lights and wheels. Large slicks for easy rolling. Size of cars 3½". Blister packed on 5" x 7½" cards. 2 dozen to carton. Weight 8 lbs.

MODEL "A" ROADSTER

1972 catalog page showing No. 2400 HOP'D RODS

1972 – 1976

$6.00/$8.00/$10.00

new! KOOL KARS

1240 KOOL KARS. 3 assorted custom racing cars with big wheels, and the real Kool "Raked Look." Die-cast metal bodies, silver painted interiors and engines. Assortment includes the Sand "Flee," "Screecher Creature," and Drag "Asp." Size of cars 2¾". Blister packed on racy style cards. 3 dozen to carton. Weight 7 lbs. Prepriced 49¢.

SAND FLEE

DRAG ASP

SCREECHER CREATURE

1972 catalog page showing No. 1240 KOOL KARS
1972 – 1975
$6.00/$8.00/$10.00

2943 Armored Cars

U. S. M-8 Armored Car
1973 – 1976
$10.00/$12.00/$15.00

British Mark II Armored Car
1973 – 1976
$10.00/$12.00/$15.00

construction rigs

LOADER

new!

ROLLER

DOZER

2935 CONSTRUCTION RIGS. Assortment includes 3 popular pieces of construction equipment. The broad blade Dozer with treads, scoop shovel Loader and heavy duty pavement Roller. All items have die-cast metal bodies and sturdy, high impact plastic chassis. Length from 4" to 5½". Blister packed on colorful construction rig card 4⅞" x 8¼". 12 each to carton. Weight 6 lbs.

TOOTSIETOY® fords

WOODY

new!

TOURING

PICK-UP

ROADSTER

3025 TOOTSIETOY FORDS. Assortment consists of the most sought after auto styles of late twenties and early thirties—The famous "Model A Fords". All cars have die-cast metal bodies and colorful high impact plastic chassis. Extreme styling care and high mold expense were necessary to reproduce the "Woody" station wagon. "Touring" sedan, "Pick-Up" truck, and "Roadster" with rumble seat. Length of item 4¼". Visually packed in display box 2¾" x 3" x 5½". 12 each to carton. Weight 7 lbs.

2935 CONSTRUCTION RIGS and 3025 TOOTSIETOY FORDS
2935 – $5.00/$10.00/$15.00
3025 – $15.00/$20.00/$25.00

1296 Army Toughs

Deuce ½ Truck
1973 – 1976
$8.00/$10.00/$12.00

U. S. Jeep
1973 – 1976
$8.00/$10.00/$12.00

German Kubelwagon
1973 – 1976
$8.00/$10.00/$12.00

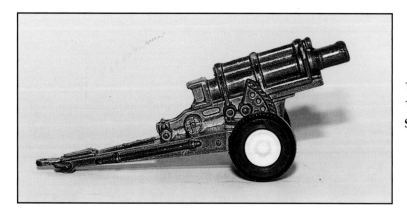

105 MM Howitzer
1973 – 1976
$2.00/$4.00/$6.00

1295 Vega Wagon
1973 – 1979
$8.00/$10.00/$12.00

1295 Gremlin
1973 – 1979
$8.00/$10.00/$12.00

Hitch-up™ Series

2524 Speed Boat
1970 – 1976
$10.00/$15.00/$20.00

2530 Kubelwagon and Cannon
1973 – 1975
$10.00/$15.00/$20.00

2537 Deuce ½ Military Truck and Trailer
1973 – 1975
$10.00/$15.00/$20.00

2538 Airstream Trailer ad Vega
1973 – 1975
$10.00/$15.00/$20.00

2539 ATC Honda Cycle and Gremlin
1973 – 1975
$15.00/$20.00/$25.00

2435 Farm Tractor
1974 – 1977
$10.00/$15.00/$20.00

2544 Camper
1974 – 1976
$10.00/$15.00/$20.00

2548 School Bus
1974 – 1977
$10.00/$15.00/$20.00

1270 Racing Cars

Ferrari #8
1974 – 1977
$8.00/$10.00/$12.00

Porche #4
1974 – 1977
$8.00/$10.00/$12.00

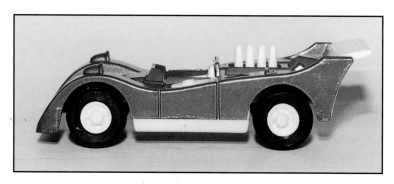

Can Am
1974 – 1977
$8.00/$10.00/$12.00

1011 Midgets added to 1974

Flat Abarth, Custom Rod, Tornado, and Dragster
1974 – 1977
$2.00/$3.00/$4.00

Roadster, Run-A-bout, Land Rover
1974 – 1977
$2.00/$3.00/$4.00

Durant® plastic car series

new!

new!

THE THING (VW)

'34 FORD "VICKY"

DESERT DEV

ANANA PEELER

ROD N' RAIL

DURANT PLASTIC

5050 "VW"-"VICKY" ASST. 12 each assorted of the following 2 cars. Weight 6 lbs.

5050 THE THING. VW latest entry in the auto world. Combines the rustic features of an "off the road" vehicle with the advantages of a standard sedan. Bright plated front and rear lights. Rag top style roof, chassis pan, big wheels combined with large scale of item, give the car the "BIG" look. Overall length 11½". 12 each, bulk packed to carton. Weight 6 lbs.

5050 34 FORD VICTORIA "5 WINDOW COUPE". The most popular auto style for '34 was the "5 window VICKY." Reproduced with all its flowing curves and graceful front plated grill. Due to its scale this coupe has the "BIG" look for plastic cars. Overall length 11½". 12 each, bulk packed to carton. Weight 6 lbs.

5011 "FUNNY CAR" ASST. 12 each assorted of the following 3 cars. Weight 6 lbs.

5011 DESERT DEVIL RECONNAISSANCE CAR. California Baja Desert fun car. A civilian revamp style of the great Mercedes military car of past fame. Extra wheels for sand traction. Lots of chrome details, wheels, radiator lights, windshield frame, rear tire cover. Overall length 11". 12 each, bulk packed to carton. Weight 6 lbs.

5011 BANANA PEELER DRAGSTER. Latest dragster with enclosed driver's seat and custom styled rear end. Plated engine, twin plated fuel tanks, sculptural body design, huge rear slicks with plated wheels, bicycle front tires with plated spokes. Overall length 12". 12 each, bulk packed to carton. Weight 6 lbs.

5011 ROD N' RAIL, EXTENDED HOT ROD. "C" cab custom style body with extended frame, make a mighty slick look for any drag track. Plated engine with chrome fuel tanks, coach lamps, and chute. Huge rear racing slicks with chrome wheels and bicycle front drag tires with chrome spokes. Overall length 10". 12 each, bulk packed to carton. Weight 6 lbs.

5025 PLASTIC CAR DISPLAY. 36 each cars packed into a shipper, shelf display.

1974 catalog page DURANT® PLASTIC CAR SERIES
$10.00/$15.00/$20.00

1297 Rescue Vehicles

Personnel Truck
1975 – 1979
$8.00/$10.00/$12.00

Equipment Truck
1975 – 1979
$8.00/$10.00/$12.00

Ambulance
1975 – 1979
$8.00/$10.00/$12.00

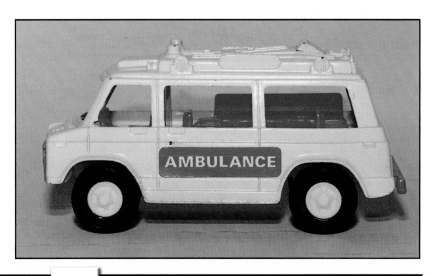

2552 Rescue Helicopter
1975 – 1979
$10.00/$15.00/$20.00

1295 Dune Buggy
1975 – 1979
$8.00/$10.00/$12.00

2527 Beach Buggy Hitch-up™
1970 – 1975
$10.00/$15.00/$20.00

1250 Tootsietoy Tiny Toughs

Van
1975 – 1979
$5.00/$10.00/$15.00

Chevy Blazer
1975 – 1979
$5.00/$10.00/$15.00

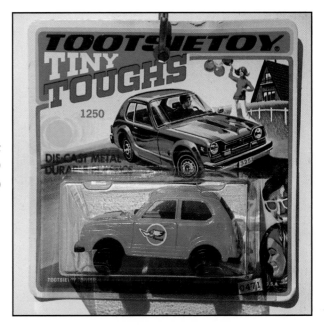

Honda Civic
1975 – 1979
$5.00/$10.00/$15.00

VW Bug
1975 – 1979
$5.00/$10.00/$15.00

Land Rover
1975 – 1979
$5.00/$10.00/$15.00

Pickup
1975 – 1979
$5.00/$10.00/$15.00

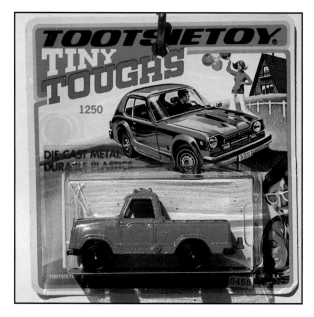

2301 Tiny Toughs Hitch-ups

Motorcycle and Trailer pulled by Van
1976 – 1979
$10.00/$15.00/$20.00

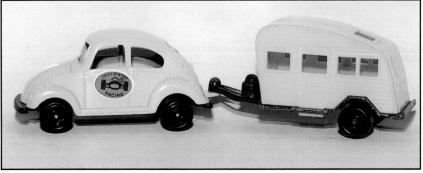

VW pulling House Trailer
1976 – 1979
$10.00/$15.00/$20.00

2302 Tiny Toughs Semis

Gravel
1976 – 1979
$10.00/$12.00/$15.00

Semi Trailer
1976 – 1979
$10.00/$15.00/$20.00

Logger
1976 – 1979
$10.00/$12.00/$15.00

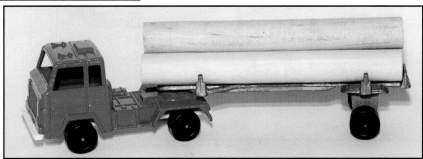

2303 Tiny Toughs Highway Vehicles

Greyhound Bus
5", 1976 – 1979
$10.00/$12.00/$15.00

Fire Truck with ladder
5", 1976 – 1979
$10.00/$15.00/$20.00

Camper with mural
1976 – 1979
$10.00/$15.00/$20.00

1299 Tootsietoy S.W.A.T. Trucks

Police Van
1976 – 1979
$6.00/$8.00/$10.00

Armored Car
1976 – 1979
$6.00/$8.00/$10.00

Special Equipment Truck
1976 – 1979
$6.00/$8.00/$10.00

2200 Sports Van
1977 – 1979
$6.00/$8.00/$10.00

2980 F-16 Plane
1977 – 1979
$10.00/$15.00/$20.00

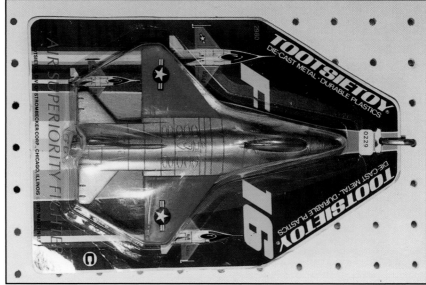

2216 Adventure Exploring Vehicle Unit
1977
$6.00/$8.00/$10.00

2220 Scorpion Helicopter
1977 – 1979
$6.00/$8.00/$10.00

2210 Special Mission Vehicles

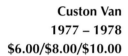

Custon Van
1977 – 1978
$6.00/$8.00/$10.00

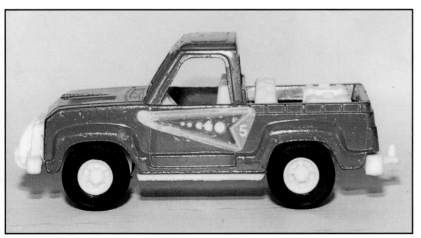

Off-road Pickup
1977 – 1979
$6.00/$8.00/$10.00

Special Equipment Truck
1977 – 1978
$6.00/$8.00/$10.00

Forward Car Truck
1977 – 1978
$6.00/$8.00/$10.00

Special Speed Racer
1977 – 1978
$6.00/$8.00/$10.00

3260 Tootsietoy Red Baron Tri-plane
1978 – 1979
$20.00/$25.00/$30.00

"Wide Body" Series

3152 Fire Truck with a Ladder
1978 – 1979
$10.00/$12.00/$15.00

3160 Sport Van with Canoe
1977 – 1978
$10.00/$12.00/$15.00

2975 Tootsietoy War Ships

Battleship
1978 – 1979
$10.00/$12.00/$15.00

Aircraft Carrier
1978 – 1979
$10.00/$12.00/$15.00

2080 Tootsietoy Sea Power

Destroyer
1978 – 1979
$10.00/$12.00/$15.00

Submarine
1978 – 1979
$10.00/$12.00/$15.00

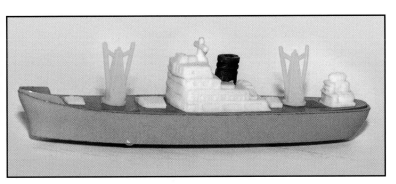

Cargo Ship
1978 – 1979
$10.00/$12.00/$15.00

2406 Tootsietoy Tow Truck
1978 – 1979
$8.00/$10.00/$12.00

2990 Keep On Trucking

Pepsi Truck Semi
1979
$15.00/$20.00/$25.00

RC Truck Semi
1979
$15.00/$20.00/$25.00

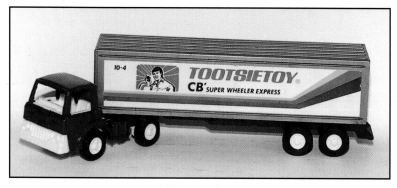

CB Truck Semi
1979
$15.00/$20.00/$25.00

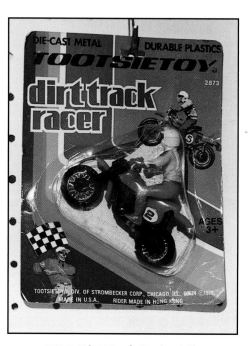

2873 Dirt Track Racing Bike
1979
$6.00/$8.00/$10.00

3140 Rover 4 x 4
1978 – 1979
$10.00/$12.00/$15.00

3140 Subaru Brat
1978 – 1979
$10.00/$12.00/$15.00

3180 Tootsietoy Dump Truck
1979
$10.00/$12.00/$15.00

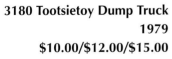

3185 Tootsietoy F4U Corsair
1979
$10.00/$15.00/$20.00

3210 Catering Truck
1979
$10.00/$15.00/$20.00

3166 Tootsietoy Sport Airplane
1979
$10.00/$15.00/$20.00

3168 Tootsietoy Blazer
1978 – 1979, side boards
$10.00/$15.00/$20.00

3168 Tootsietoy Blazer
1978 – 1979, no side boards
$10.00/$12.00/$15.00

3151 Emergency Rescue Truck
1978 – 1979
$10.00/$12.00/$15.00

3152 Fire Truck
1978 – 1979
$10.00/$12.00/$15.00

3150 TV News Helicopter
1978 – 1979
$10.00/$12.00/$15.00

3205 Tootsietoy Soft Drink Truck (RC)
1979
$15.00/$20.00/$25.00

5014 36 Ford "Cruzin" Coupe
1979
$6.00/$8.00/$10.00

3185 Tootsietoy Air Races
1979
$25.00/$35.00/$45.00

2872 Tootsietoy "Flash Gordon" Star Ships

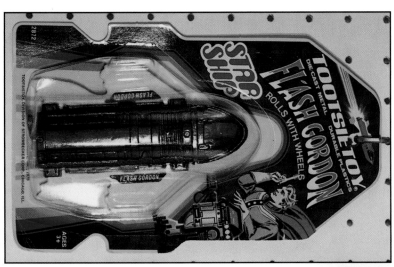

Ming Space Ship
1978 – 1979
$15.00/$20.00/$25.00

Flash Gordon Space Ship
1978 – 1979
$15.00/$20.00/$25.00

Packaged Toys and Boxed Sets
1970 – 1979

Tootsietoy had various methods of packaging their brightly painted and decorated toys. The early 1970, No. 1290 and No. 1295 car and truck assortments were packed in a clear, stackable, blister case with a printed roadway base. This was changed in 1971 to a brightly illustrated card. Cars and trucks were packed under a clear, blister case for easy display.

The many boxed sets of toys were often placed in a white plastic tray, bordered by colorful cardboard, and then completely sealed with a plastic or cellophane-type material.

A single toy or boxed set in its original packaging will usually add 15 to 20 percent to the price of the toy or sets. Strombecker produced over 90 different packaged sets between 1970 and 1979. Some are rather scarce today because they were only produced in limited numbers and carried for one or two years in the Strombecker toy catalogs of the 1970s.

The following pages will illustrate some examples of Tootsietoys in their original packaging.

1055 Swedish Jet
1970
$20.00

1290 Dune Buggy
1970
$20.00

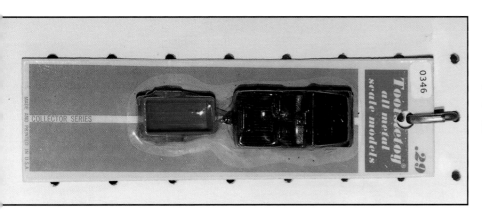

1438 Jeep and Trailer
1970
$20.00

1682 Construction Set
1970
$45.00

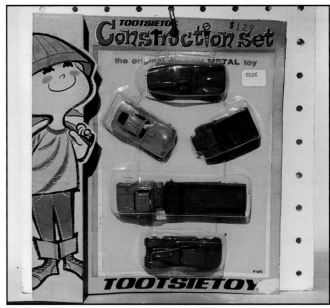

1249 "Little" Toughs all Dated 1971

Flatbed with Jaguar
$25.00

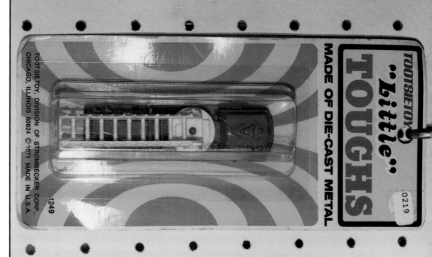

Ladder Truck
$25.00

Hydraulic Crane
$30.00

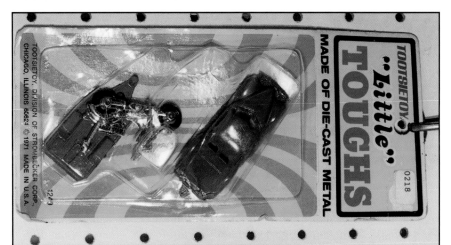

40 Ford motorcycle, and Trailer
$25.00

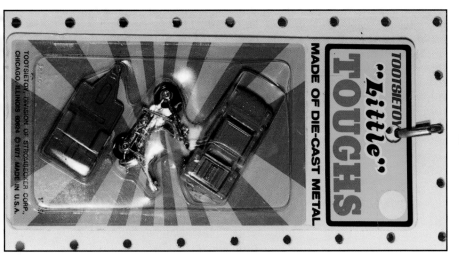

Dune Buggy, Motorcycle, and Trailer
$25.00

Jeep, Boat, and Trailer
$25.00

Dune Buggy, Boat, and Trailer
$25.00

Log Truck
$25.00

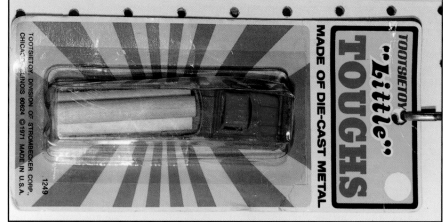

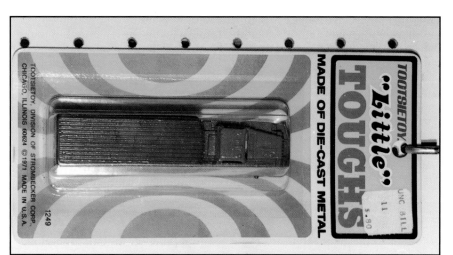

Semi Van Trailer Truck
$25.00

2415 Jet Launch
1972
$35.00

3100 Super Twist
1975
$30.00

3100 Dragster
1972
$35.00

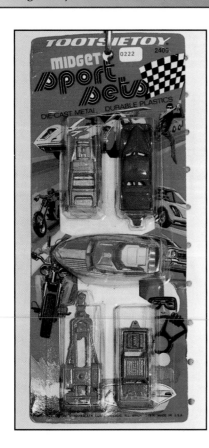

2405 Midget Sports Set
1974
$25.00

2552 Rescue Chopper
$30.00

2220 Scorpion Chopper
1976
$20.00

2080 War Ships 1978

Cargo Ship
$25.00

Destroyer Ship
$25.00

Submarine
$25.00

1295 Exxon Oil
1977 – 1979
$20.00

1295 Forestry Truck
1977 – 1979
$20.00

1299 S.W.A.T. Van
1976
$20.00

1732 Spearhead Set
1973
$75.00

1745 Hitch-ups™
1971
$75.00

1760 Sportsters
1971
$100.00

No. 3195 Tanker Truck
6", 1979
$35.00

No. 3210 Catering Truck
6", 1979
$35.00

No. 3223 Canoe Hitch-up
10½", 1979, rare
$65.00

No. 3181 Tootsietoy Bulldozer
5", 1979
$15.00/$20.00/$25.00

No. 2020 CHOO*CHOO Train
12", 1969
$55.00

No. 1705 Camper Combo
9", 1972, rare
$65.00

No. 3020 Ford Touring Sedan
5", 1974
$25.00

No. 3020 Ford Roadster
5", 1974
$25.00

No. 3020 Ford Pick-up Truck
5", 1974
$25.00

No. 3020 Ford Woody Station Wagon
5", 1974
$25.00

No. 2522 Tootsietoy K-9 Hitch-up
1969 –1970, rare
$75.00

No. 2526 Jungle Cage Hitch-up
1969 only, very rare, with/lion or tiger
$85.00

No. 1451 Farm Tractor & Wagon
1968 – 1969
$45.00

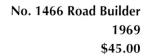

No. 1452 Hydraulic Crane
1968 – 1969
$40.00

No. 1466 Road Builder
1969
$45.00

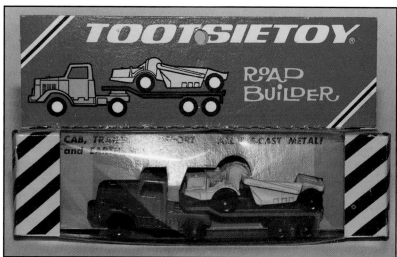

No. 1456 Truck & Cycle
1968 – 1969
$45.00

No. 1457 Power Shovel
1968 – 1969
$40.00

No. 1469 Truck & Horse Trailer
1969
$45.00

No. 1460 Auto Transport
1968 – 1969
$55.00

No. 1463 Safari Hunt
1968 – 1969
$50.00

No. 1464 Carousel Truck
1968, rarest in series
$75.00

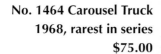

No. 1465 Livestock Transport
1968 – 1969, four cows
$50.00

No. 1465 Livestock Transport
1968 – 1969, four horses
$50.00

No. 1467 House Boat and Transporter
1969
$45.00

No. 1468 Car and Cabin Cruiser
1969, all types of cars
$45.00

1801 Starbase Zeus
1977
$100.00

This section consists of all the boxed and packaged sets produced between 1970 and 1979. The number for each set is the actual catalog number taken from original catalogs. You will find the years they were in production beside each set. At this time there are no prices available. However, prices should be between $25.00 and $100.00 depending on the availability of each set.

1640 TOOTSIETOY CONSTRUCTION SET: 1979
Set contains dump truck, 4 x 4 pickup, and bulldozer, Also included are four small pylons and two road block signs.

1642 TOOTSIETOY EMERGENCY SET: 1979
Set contains wide body police and fire truck, helicopter, and four action figures.

1654 TOOTSIETOY SPORT SET: 1979
Set contains sport truck wide body pulling two motorcycles on a trailer. A tough 4 x 4 pulling four canoes on a special trailer.

1665 TOOTSIETOY TOLLWAY SET: 1979
Set contains two wide body die-cast metal trucks, four highway pylons, and a highly detailed two-station operating toll plaza.

1666 TOOTSIETOY DIRT BIKE SET: 1979
Set contains two wide body die-cast vehicles, two dirt bikes, dirt bike trailer, and two plastic riders.

1667 TOOTSIETOY CATERING & SOFT DRINK SET: 1979
Set contains two different wide-body trucks: catering with two small plastic cases and soft drink truck with two small cases and two small carts.

1686 FARM EQUIPMENT SET: 1970 – 1971
Set contains a heavy-duty tractor with high rear fenders, four unit disc harrow, double shear plow, and utility wagon.

1689 AIRPORT SET: 1970 – 1972
Set contains cast metal airplane, gas tanker, landing Jeep, Jeepster car, and Jeep truck.

1690 TRUCK FLEET SET: 1970 – 1972
Set contains logger, cab and semi-trailer, Jeep truck, three logs, and six barrels.

1691 FIRE FIGHTING SET: 1970 – 1972
Set contains aerial ladder truck, emergency Jeep, first aid panel truck, pumper, chief's car, and badge.

1692 CONSTRUCTION SET: 1970 – 1972
Set contains skip loader, earth mover, cab with equipment trailer, Jeep, and low side shuttle truck.

1694 CAR FLEET SET: 1970 – 1971
Set contains six die-cast cars and trucks and boat and trailer.

1704 CROSS COUNTRY SET: 1970 – 1972
Set contains 14 pieces: nine cars and trucks, midget race racer trailer, boat with trailer, and game spinner.

1704 TRAFFIC CONTROL SET: 1970 – 1972
Set contains two choppers, police badge, four cars Honda cycle, transport unit with cab, and game spinner.

1705 CAMPER COMBO SET: 1971 – 1973
Set contains a new "Pop Top" camper hitched to a new Super Clicks™ car.

1711 STARBASE SET: 1977 – 1978
Set consists of the following: Major Mars space figure shuttle craft spaceship, all-terrain vehicle, and AT trailer.

1712 BIO-TRONIC MAN: 1977 – 1978
Set consists of the following: Bio-Tronic Man figure, Tootsietoy truck, motorcycle, and motorcycle trailer.

1714 CAPT. LAZER
Set consists of the following: Capt. Lazer hero figure, Tootsietoy car, watercraft with trailer.

1722 TOOTSIETOY TINY TOUGHS CAR SET: 1975 – 1977
Set contains a camping trailer, fishing boat with trailer motorcycle with trailer, and two die-cast metal pulling trucks.

1723 TOOTSIETOY RV, RECREATION VEHICLE SET 1976 – 1977
Set contains a camping trailer, fishing boat with trailer motorcycle with trailer, and two die-cast metal pulling trucks.

1724 TOOTSIETOY "KEEP ON TRUCKING" SET 1976 – 1978
Set contains semi trailer truck with pulling cab, logger truck and gravel hauler trailer truck.

1730 GRAND PRIX RACING SET: 1974 – 1975
Set contains five European race circuit cars: Ferrari, Porsche Can Am, and two Custom Team Racers.

1731 OPEN ROAD CAMPING SET: 1973 – 1979
Set contains camping trailer, Vega station wagon, run-a-bout outboard boat, die-cast boat trailer; also Gremlin car and Suzuki dirt bike.

1732 SPEARHEAD MILITARY SET: 1973 – 1977
Set contains seven pieces of military items: Kubelwagon car, 105mm Howitzer cannon, deuce ½ Army truck with missle rest, two LaCross missiles, Army Jeep, and trailer.

1733 TOOTSIETOY CALIFORNIA FUN TIME: 1979
Set contains hang glider action with two sports figures, custom van, off road pickup truck, fun wagon, and floatable raft.

1736 TOOTSIETOY JET FLIGHT SET: 1979
Set contains F-16 Jet Fighter serviced for flight by fuel truck, utility truck, crew transport, and support trailer.

1740 TRAVEL SET: 1970 – 1972
Set contains a six piece hitch together train, two modern jets, six die-cast cars, a speed boat, and three pump gas island.

1741 PLAYTIME SET: 1970 – 1972
Set contains both aerial ladder and pumper fire trucks, helicopter, construction vehicles, pickup, oil tanker, Jeep, earth mover, shuttle truck, panel truck, Jeepster, tow truck, and four cars.

1742 TOOTSIETOY S.W.A.T. GIFT SET: 1976 – 1977
Set contains three vehicles, search light, and four S.W.A.T. plastic figures.

1745 HITCH-UP ™ SET: 1970 – 1979
Set contains various vehicles pulling boat, cycle, and other metal vehicles. All years contain different vehicles.

1746 ROADMASTER JR. SET: 1972 – 1979
Set contains auto transport trailer and modern cab with windows. Three die-cast cars or trucks with two additional cars for transport trailer.

1747 FIRE FIGHTERS SET: 1970 – 1979
Set contains aerial ladder, die-cast fire truck, chemical truck, pumper truck with two ladders, and chief's badge.

1748 FARM SET: 1970 – 1979
Set contains farm tractor and spreader cart, horse van trailer unit with six horses, and runabout truck.

1749 TOOTSIETOY EMERGENCY "RESCUE 1" SET: 1975 – 1979
Set contains four exciting rescue vehicles and the Bell "Jet Ranger" Helicopter.

1750 ACTIVITY GARAGE SET: 1970 – 1971
Set contains Super Service Station with action carwash, grease ramp, six gas pumps, and four cars or trucks.

1750 TOOTSIETOY "AMERICAN ROAD" SET: 1976 – 1977
Set contains three die-cast pulling cars, motorcycle with trailer, fishing boat with boat trailer, camping trailer, and a Winnebago RV Vehicle.

1751 SUPER AIRPORT SET: 1970 – 1971
Set contains three die-cast airplanes, hangar, and action control panel with hand throttle.

1753 CHOPPER SET: 1972 – 1973
Set contains three latest style hogs. Trikes are "Kraut Chopper," "Black Knight," and "Myster Hogger."

1754 STARBASE BETA SET: 1977 – 1978
Set consists of Major Mars figure, the android Zoltan, starship space craft, shuttle craft spaceship, two all-terrain vehicles, and ATV trailer.

1756 CHALLENGER DRAGSTER SET: 1972 – 1973
Set contains two 8" long dragsters: "Stars and Bars Special" and the "Inch Pincher."

1758 BIO-TRONIC MAN 11 SET: 1977 – 1978
Set consists of the following: Bio-Tronic Man, F-16 airplane, equipment truck, forward cab pickup truck, and motorcycle with trailer.

1759 CAPT. LAZER AND THE GREAT APE: 1977 – 1978
Set consists of the following: Capt. Lazer, the Great Ape, Capt. Lazer's car, custom van, truck, pickup, watercraft with trailer.

1760 SPORTSTER SET: 1971 – 1979
Set contains 13 pieces including the Attex, two Honda motorcycles with trailer, dune buggy, boat with trailer, Snow Cat snowmobile, and four rough-going trucks.

1762 TOOTSIETOY FORDS: 1974 – 1976
Set contains four famous Model A Fords. Extreme stying care and high mold expense went to produce the Woody station wagon, Touring sedan, pickup truck, and Roadster with rumble seats.

1764 TOOTSIETOY TASK FORCE 88 SET: 1978 – 1979
Set contains battleship, aircraft carrier, destroyer, cargo ship, and submarine.

1765 ARMORED PATROL MILITARY SET: 1973 – 1976
Set contains two die-cast armored cars, Kubelwagen, 105mm Howitzer cannon, Army truck, Army Jeep, and deuce ½ truck with missle rest and LaCross missile.

1768 THE TOOTSIETOY CONSTRUCTION CO. SET: 1974 – 1976
Set contains dozer, roller, loader, and three other construction vehicles.

1770 "BIG SLICKS" ATV HITCH UP SET: 1972
Set contains large die-cast car with large wheels pulling a trailer with an off-the-road vehicle on it.

1772 "BIG SLICKS" TRAIL BIKE HITCH UP SET: 1972 – 1974
Set contains large die-cast car, a trailer, two Honda #70 Trail Bikes.

1775 "BIG SLICKS" CHOPPER HITCH UP SET: 1972 – 1973

Set contains large die-cast metal car with three wheel die-cast metal chopper and metal trailer.

1780 EXCLUSIVE TOOTSIETOY SERVICE STATION CARRYING CASE: 1970 – 1971

Set contains service station that folds out within its own case. A car ramp and 10 cars and trucks. Case has its own handle on side.

1790 TOOTSIETOY "CB" HIGHWAY SET: 1977 – 1979

Set contains all the latest highway equipment associated with the CB craze. Large express semi-trailer/tractor truck rig, California van, 2-wheeler Honda motorcycle with trailer, Smokey Bear Police car, large camper, police "spy in the sky" helicopter, and CB microphone with push button action.

1792 TOOTSIETOY POLICE SET: 1978 – 1979

Set contains van, special equipment van, police personnel truck, emergency truck, search light, helicopter, motorcycle, badge, and two road block barricades.

1793 TOOTSIETOY FLASH GORDON C SET: 1978 – 1979

Set contains popular movie and T.V. heros featured in action space set. Included are "Flash Gordon" starship, "Ming" starship, two surface explorer vehicles with two trailers, Flash Gordon, Ming, and Dale plastic figures.

1800 TOOTSIETOY LARGE S.W.A.T. GIFT SET: 1976 – 1977

Set contains the complete "Special Weapons and Tactics" team vehicle set, a helicopter, three plastic figures, moveable search light, and five different 4" S.W.A.T. trucks.

1801 STARBASE ZEUS: 1977 – 1978

Set made of high impact material, quality molded, playset components for space station platform. Set has two figures and five vehicles.

1802 BIO-TRONIC LABORATORY: 1977 – 1978

Set made of high impact material, quality molded playset components for Bio-Tronic Lab, complete with Tootsietoy die-cast metal vehicles.

1803 CAPT. LAZER'S SECRET HIDEOUT: 1977 – 1978

Set made of high impact material, quality molded playset components for secret hideout, grid system layout for various playset arrangements. Set has two figures and five different vehicles.

1805 TOOTSIETOY FAIR ACRES FARM SET: 1970

Set contains realistic two-story barn, fenced coral holds two horses, two pigs, two cows, and one chicken, farm tractor, disc harrow, plow, utility wagon, Jeep truck, pickup truck, overland Jeep, and skip loader.

1805 TOOTSIETOY "INTERSTATE" SET: 1976 – 1979

Set contains the complete highway set. Includes four pulling metal cars, Greyhound bus, semi trailer truck, logger truck and gravel hauler truck.

1810 TOOTSIETOY FIRE STATION SET: 1970

Set contains plastic fire station, snorkel truck, pumper, panel truck, fire chief's badge, net, ladders, fire axes, and stretcher

1815 TOOTSIETOY FIGHTER COMMAND SET: 1979

Set contains highly detailed WWII Fighter serviced for missions by fuel truck, utility truck, crew transport, and support trailer, four military figures and transporter guard ground operations.

1830 TOOTSIETOY EMERGENCY "RESCUE 2" SET: 1975 – 1978

Set contains two Bell "Jet Ranger" rescue helicopters, paramedic ambulance, equipment truck, personnel truck, aerial ladder truck, and three other popular service trucks.

1835 TOOTSIETOY FLYING PATROL: 1979

Set contains B-26 Marauder Bomber, F4U Corsair, and P-40 Flying Tiger.

1840 "ROAD MASTER" SET: 1970 – 1977

Set contains auto transport with two cars, horse van with six horses, logger with three logs, and six other 4" toys.

1850 SUPER CONSTRUCTION SET: 1974 – 1978

Set contains broad blade dozer, loader, roller, dump truck, cement truck, and four other 4" construction trucks.

1858 TOOTSIETOY MOTO-CROSS CYCLE SET: 1978 – 1979

Set contains three die-cast metal frame motocross dirt bikes with rubber tires plus three flexible vinyl motocross drivers that attach to handlebars and footrests, large die-cast metal wide body sport truck and cycle trailer, two large jump and hill climb track sections complete the set.

1860 SUPER SLICKS™ "6 PACK" SET: 1971 – 1974

Set contains Panzer Wagon, Bandito, Desert Fox, Pie Wagon, Twin Shaft, and the Dune Buster. Die-cast metal body is painted in show colors.

1862 TOOTSIETOY "CAREFREE DAYS" SET: 1979

Set includes Blazer pickup truck with camper top, Blazer pickup with side boards, Blazer 4 x 4 pick-up, ATV vehicle, canoe trailer with two canoes, boat with die-cast metal trailer.

1865 TOOTSIETOY SUPER SPORT SET: 1977 – 1979

Set contains two Scorpion helicopters, California van, large camper, two Honda motorcycles with trailer, Gremlin, speed boat and trailer, Jeepster, medium size motorcycle with trailer, Jeep, pickup truck, all-terrain vehicle, VW, Zodiac boat with trailer, and Bronco truck.

1870 TOOTSIETOY "BIG SPORT" SET: 1973 – 1976

Set contains 19 different pieces: the speed boat, boat trailer, camper trailer, dirt bike, snowmobile with trailer, two Honda twin bikes with trailer, Attex, 3-wheeler, beach buggy, Jeepster, Bronco, Vega, Gremlin, Jeep, pickup, and VW bug.

1875 TOOTSIETOY EMERGENCY VEHICLE SET: 1977 – 1978

Set contains 12 fire, police, and rescue vehicles, search light trailer, large helicopter, aerial ladder trucks, and eight various figures of rescue and fire personnel.

1872 TOOTSIETOY ROAD MASTER SET: 1978 – 1979

Set consists of the following die-cast metal vehicles: tow truck, semi trailer rig, logger rig, auto transport with two cars, and eight other popular 4" cars and trucks.

2085 CAR CARRIER: 1970

Set contains semi cab with car trailer, three Playmates vehicles with plastic removable drivers.

1985 CAR CARRIER: 1970

Set contains semi cab with car trailer, three Playmates vehicles with plastic removable drivers.

2090 MOTHER GOOSE: 1970

Hand-decorated Mother Goose nods her head when pulled. Peter's wife rides in a take-apart pumpkin. All the subjects are mounted on die-cast metal bases with sturdy hooks.

2405 MIDGET SPORT SETS: 1974 – 1979

Set contains five different items in each set. Theme of sets range from car racing, recreation, and general sports.

2831 BLISTER CARDED "JAM PAC™": 1971 – 1979

Set contains eight different cars and trucks packed under a clear, case style, blister.

2834 TOOTSIETOY "JAM PAC™ FLEET": 1970 – 1973

Set contains eight die-cast metal cars and trucks and a set of three gas pumps on an island.

2835 TOOTSIETOY "JAM PAC™" SET: 1970 – 1971

Set contains 10 top selling die-cast cars and trucks.

2850 JET FIGHTERS SET: 1970 – 1977

Set contains three die-cast airplanes: models of Swedish Saab J 35 "Dragon," U.S. Northrop F 5A "Little Tiger," West German McDonnel F4C "Phantom 11," and French Dassault 111C "Mirage."

2855 TRAIN SET: 1970 – 1971

Set contains six-piece, highly detailed train. Cars include diesel engine, coal car, reefer, covered hopper, cattle car, and caboose.

2870 TOOTSIETOY CAR AND BOAT HITCH-UP® ASSORTMENT: 1978 – 1979

Includes two different blister carded items. Each item has a die-cast metal car or truck with die-cast metal boat trailers and boats.

2871 TOOTSIE TOY CAR AND MOTORCYCLE HITCH-UP® ASSORTMENT: 1978 – 1979

Includes two different blister carded items. Each item has a die-cast metal car or truck, die-cast metal cycle trailer, cycles with rubber tires and plated finishes.

2977 TOOTSIETOY JET FORMATION: 1979

Set contains three all die-cast metal jet planes with steel axles and wheels. Each jet has a bright silver finish and colorful labels. Item length is 3".

5024 STROMBECKER "FAT KAT" HITCH-UPS: 1976 – 1978

Assortment of two well-known Hitch Up combinations. High performance ski boat with boat trailer and "FAT KAT" pulling car. Motorcycle with sculptured trailer and "FAT KAT" pulling car.

5800 TOOTSIETOY BATTERY OPERATED ELECTRIC TRAIN: 1970 – 1971

Set contains engine and three cars, 10 pieces of curved track, two sections straight track, and battery box with two forward speeds plus reverse, connecting wires and track cups.

About the Author

I always enjoyed my Tootsietoys as a small child. I joined the United States Army in 1962, and served my country in Germany for three years. Returning home in 1965, I happened to discover one small Tootsietoy CJ3 Army Jeep in an old desk drawer. This, I later found out, was the sole survivor from my childhood. I wanted to gather more toys and start a collection of America's first die-cast toys.

I started attending antique shows and the larger toy shows to search out and purchase more Tootsietoys to build a nice collection. The only regret I have is not buying the pre-war toys first. But making only $2.36 an hour at a power plant in 1965 did limit my buying power somewhat. Along with rent, utilities, and insurances, I did however still manage to buy a few toys when I could spare the extra cash.

Thirty nine years later at age 60, I still enjoy this rewarding popular hobby of collecting Tootsietoys and learning new information about them every day. I am still searching for the small handful of items I lack for a complete collection of Tootsietoys.

All the toys and boxed sets pictured in my new third edition book are from my own personal collection, with the exception of the few photographs supplied by fellow collectors or toys lent to me to photograph for this book.

Happy collecting!

David E. Richter
Above photo taken at St. Louis, Missouri, Toy Museum several years ago while on vacation.

Tootsietoy Check List

Now available, the first pocket-size Tootsietoy Collector's Check List with a complete description of each toy and space available to record grade, color, tire type, value, and price paid. This Tootsietoy Collector's Check List will provide you with an accurate record of your collection and items wanted in this handy 5¼" x 3½" 63 page book. Special $5.00. Send to:

David E. Richter
6817 Sutherland
Mentor, OH 44060

TOY	DESCRIPTION	GRADE	COLOR	TIRES	VALUE	COST
	AIRCRAFT & SPACESHIPS					
	#4482 Bleriot (Large)					
	#4491 Bleriot (Small)					
	#4650 Biplane					
	#4660 Aero-Dawn					
	#4660 Aero-Dawn					
	#106 Low Wing					
	#107 High Wing					
	#4649 Ford Tri-Motor					
	#4649 Ford Tri-Motor					
	#4675 Bi-Wing					
	#4675 Bi-Wing					
	#4675 Bi-Wing Seaplane					
	#4660 Seaplane					
	#4659 Autogyro					
	#4659 Autogyro					
	#720 Fly-N-Gyro					
	#119 US Army Plane					
	#119 (Camouflaged)					
	#717 DC-2 TWA					
	#717 (Two-Tone)					
	#718 Waco Bomber					
	#718 (Camouflaged)					
	#718 Waco Dive Bomber					
	#718 (Camouflaged)					
	NOTES:					

2   3

Inside pages of Tootsietoy check list

Index